A New Beginning

PETER LANG
New York • Washington, D.C./Baltimore
Bern • Frankfurt am Main • Berlin • Vienna • Paris

Shirley Kolack

A New Beginning

The Jews of Historic Lowell, Massachusetts

PETER LANG
New York • Washington, D.C./Baltimore
Bern • Frankfurt am Main • Berlin • Vienna • Paris

Library of Congress Cataloging-in-Publication Data
Kolack, Shirley.
A new beginning: the Jews of historic Lowell,
Massachusetts/ Shirley Kolack.
p. cm
Includes bibliographical references.
1. Jews—Massachusetts—Lowell—History. 2. Lowell
(Mass.)—Ethnic relations. I. Title.
F74.L9K65   305.8'92407444—dc20   96-41811
ISBN 0-8204-2263-0

Die Deutsche Bibliothek-CIP-Einheitsaufnahme
Kolack, Shirley.
A new beginning: the Jews of historic Lowell,
Massachusetts/ Shirley Kolack. – New York; Washington,
D.C./Baltimore; Bern; Frankfurt am Main; Berlin; Vienna;
Paris: Lang.
ISBN 0-8204-2263-0

Photograph on the front cover courtesy The Lowell Museum.

© 1997 Peter Lang Publishing, Inc., New York

All rights reserved.
Reprint or reproduction, even partially, in all forms such as microfilm,
xerography, microfiche, microcard, and offset strictly prohibited.

To Sol and my grandchildren

Joshua, David, Michael, Jacob and Rebecca,

who represent a new beginning.

TABLE OF CONTENTS

PREFACE		xi
Chapter 1	INTRODUCTION	1
Chapter 2	SETTLEMENT PATTERNS	7
Chapter 3	ORGANIZATIONS	17
Chapter 4	OCCUPATIONAL PATTERNS	31
Chapter 5	ADAPTATION	49
Chapter 6	PRESENT STATUS AND THE FUTURE	63
Chapter 7	THE SAGA OF AN IMMIGRANT FAMILY	75
PHOTOGRAPHS		83
INDEX		97

PHOTOGRAPHS

Original Jewish Cemetery	84
A Russian Jewish Couple	85
Early Synagogues	86
Lowell Young Men's Hebrew Association	87
Mogan David Baseball Team	88
The Highland Club	89
New Lowell Hebrew Community Center and Temple Beth El	90
Street Procession to New Montefiore Synagogue	91
New Montefiore Synagogue	92
Lighting the Chanukah Menorah	93
Founding of Israel Ceremony	94
Holocaust Torah	95
Passover Seder Table	96

PREFACE

The germ of the idea for recounting the story of the historic Jewish community of Lowell came from an exhibit I co-directed on Jewish life mounted in the Mogan Cultural Center (1989) for the Lowell Historic Preservation Commission. The exhibit provided a glimpse of the rich life Jews experienced in this city, which was the birthplace of the Industrial Revolution in America. It seemed appropriate that a written record of the Jewish group should also be provided. I have attempted to document the human story of the part Jews played in the unfolding of the saga of the development of the city of Lowell as well as to place the Lowell Jewish community within the larger context of American Jewry.

My writing and research were made possible by a cultural grant from the Lowell Historic Preservation Commission, U.S. Department of the Interior for which I am grateful. I wish also to acknowledge the prior work, research and design for the exhibit on Jewish life of my colleagues Mark Levine and Nina Pattek, which provided a backdrop for this study. I also appreciate the extensive cooperation of members of the Jewish community in Lowell. Stella Klesaris was immensely helpful in graciously and efficiently word processing this manuscript.

Shirley Kolack
Lowell, Massachusetts
January, 1996

Chapter 1
INTRODUCTION

When it was founded in the early 19th century, Lowell, Massachusetts, came to symbolize what industrial capitalism could achieve—Lowell was the first American city created as an economic industrial enterprise. It was here that the manufacture of cotton textile goods was first produced on a large urban scale using machines powered by water - the Pawtucket Falls of the Merrimack River. Between the 1840s and 1920s, tens of thousands of European immigrants came to Lowell to work in the mills. Nowhere in the country was the proportion of foreign born to the total population higher than in the Merrimack Valley area.[1] Lowell became the quintessential multi-ethnic city of melting pot ideology—including the conflicts and lack of melting that this mythology obscures.[2] The melting pot theory is diminished by the lack of a simple American identity.

None of the ethnic groups were ever completely absorbed into the dominant English Protestant way of life that prevailed in Lowell for over a hundred years. Complete ethnic blending did not occur nor did complete ethnic pluralism remain. A common language and system of education have not wiped out cultural and religious distinctions. It is still possible for life to be lived within the confines of an ethnic community. For many, religious practices, family and work remain intertwined. Group identity is often maintained by acts of conscious and deliberate choice. In Lowell, the melting pot theory has proved to be inadequate as an explanation for group interrelations and problems of adjustment to American society.

From the city's founding in 1826 to 1836 Lowell's population grew from 2,500 to 18,000. As the output of the mills expanded, immigrant labor from Europe began to replace the Protestant "mill girls" from rural New England who were the initial work force. By 1900, the population had grown to over 100,000 and 40 percent of the population were foreign-born. All came to escape some form of religious persecution, political oppression, or economic hardship in their countries of origin. The large immigration of Irish in the early decades was followed by the French Canadians in the 1860s–80s. Immigrants from Southern and Eastern European countries began arriving in the 1870s. Among this group were Jews from Russia, Russia-controlled Poland and Lithuania escaping the tyranny of Czarist pogroms and poverty. Another compelling factor for immigration was that as early as 1827, young Jewish men were forceably conscripted into the Czarist army and made to serve far away from their homes for up to twenty-five years. The Russian government's intention was that over time these young men would become Russified and would convert to the Russian Orthodox faith.[3]

On May 3, 1882, the Russian government promulgated the infamous May Laws designed to bring a quick and total solution to the "Jewish problem." One third of the Jewish population was to be converted, one third forced to emigrate and one third exterminated by starvation.[4] By the 1880s, the situation in Russia was desperate and there began a major immigration of Jews to Lowell and other cities in the United States, continuing past World War I and ending only with the passage in 1924 of the Johnson Act, a restrictive, quota-based immigration law. This law combined anti-immigrant sentiment with the isolationism that followed World War I. Between 1800 and 1924, approximately two and a half million Jews immigrated into the U.S.[5]

A small group of German Jews arrived in Lowell soon after its founding. They came seeking political freedom in the wake of the German nationalist revolutions of 1830 and 1848. These Jews were mostly of middle class origin. The first to arrive in 1832 was Franklin Abels, who worked for a brief period as an overseer in the mills of the Middlesex Company. German Jews worked in the mills but soon began to create business establishments and assumed ancillary occupations that supported the growing mill economy. The Abels are listed in the Lowell city directories as merchants in gloves and hosiery, the Marks as tailors, the Wileskis as clerk, constable, and lawyer.[6] They were adherents of the new reform denomination of Judaism and, in Lowell, worshipped as Universalists. The only visible remains of this German group is a single marker that designates the burial plot of the Abels and Marks family members in the Edson burial ground within the Lowell Cemetery. They did not establish synagogues or celebrate Jewish holidays. It was only with the arrival of the Jews from Eastern Europe in the 1870s that a viable Jewish community came into existence.

These Jews of Eastern European origin have maintained a continuing presence in Lowell. Though never more than 2,000 in number, they played an important role in the city's development. The chapters that follow will explore how the Jewish immigrant experience complemented, as well as contrasted, with that of the other ethnic groups. We will explore the various phases of Jewish life in Lowell and extend its application to American Jewry generally, as well as to other ethnic groups. Immigrant Jews became Americans and, more specifically, Lowellians, while still retaining their own identity. They remained concerned with local, national, and international Jewish life. How Jews living in satellite communities of large urban areas, such as Lowell in relation to Boston, were shaped by this new experience as they struggled and persevered should prove applicable to the history of other ethnic groups as well as to new immigrants. We will explore continuity and change in their traditions and activities. Areas probed are the location and purpose of settlement patterns; occupational patterns and changes over time; the establishment of self-help organizations and their significance; adjustment patterns; and the status of the Jewish community today.

An overall theme is to capture the texture of growing up Jewish in Lowell and to uncover the linkages and relationships between Jews and other ethnic groups. The book will probe where their adaptive paths converged and were similar as well as where they diverged and were distinctive, focusing on the Jewish group's values and life circumstances that produced these results. A dilemma for Jews, as well as for other immigrant groups, was the question of balancing their traditional rituals and customs while adapting to the growing industrialized culture of America. Most had left pre-industrial villages of Europe for a burgeoning technological society.

Lowell today has special significance for the Lowell National Historical Park (1978). It has been established to keep alive the heritage of this city where the Industrial Revolution began and where a workforce of immigrants from all over Europe flocked to make their way. One of the park's missions is to supply the human face and voice of this industrial city by recounting the experiences of the ethnic groups that played a vital role in its development. In the chapters that follow the story of the part that Jews played in this process will be told. Case studies of representative Jewish families over generations will provide a personal and human focus.

First we must put in context the fact that American Jewish history is similar to the history of all the European poor who settled here. As Arthur Hertzberg indicates in *The Jews in America*, their story is a tale of a society created in a new land where the poor were unrestrained by the rigid class structure of Europe. The Jewish immigrants had unique success in America, in the land that they called golden.

Poverty and anti-Semitism were the motivating forces for most of them to leave the old world. Today most American Jews are now three or four generations removed from their immigrant origins. They live in a society which is more open to Jews than any before in the long history of the Diaspora. Memories of first generation immigrant life and past years of anti-Semitism are fading.[7] Therefore, it is fitting that the experiences of Jews in various American communities be told—their past, present and possibilities in the future.

Notes

1. Donald Cole, *Immigrant City* (Chapel Hill: University of North Carolina Press, 1963) p. 11.

2. Marc Scott Miller, *The Irony of Victory: World War II and Lowell, Massachusetts* (Chicago: University of Illinois Press,1988) p. viii.

3. Nathan Ausubel, *The Book of Jewish Knowledge* (New York: Crown Publishers, Inc., 1964) pp. 343-345.

4. Ausubel, p. 345.

5. Sidney Goldstein and Calvin Goldscheider, *Jewish Americans:Three Generations in a Jewish Community* (New Jersey: Prentice-Hall, 1968) p. 234.

6. Frederick W. Coburn, *History of Lowell and its People*, Vol. I (New York: Lewis Historical Publications) 1920.

7. Arthur Hertzberg, *The Jews in America: Four Centuries of an Uneasy Encounter* (New York: Simon and Schuster, 1989) pp. 13-14.

Chapter 2

SETTLEMENT PATTERNS

Eastern European Jews came into the city first as a trickle and later in the 1880s and 1890s as a tide. They were part of an overall exodus of Jews from the Russian and Austro-Hungarian empires, fleeing rapidly deteriorating conditions for Jews. They settled within walking distance of the large textile mills that lined the Merrimack River. This district, close by the train station, was known as The Hale-Howard Street area. It was a close knit neighborhood referred to by its inhabitants in Yiddish as a "kleine shtetl" (a little village). Initially most of the Jews came to work in the mills. They were basically a working-class group unlike the earlier German Jews who had backgrounds in commerce. Lowell was a booming industrial city. Some came directly from New York as part of a planned settlement program of the Industrial Removal Board and the United Hebrew Charities of New York established in 1874 to place Jews in towns away from large cities. Initially American Jews of German descent endeavored to divert the flow of Russian refugees from the port cities. Although sympathetic to the plight of the immigrants, the Germans worried that these newcomers would threaten their own hard-won status and fuel the fires of ever present anti-Semitism.[1]

In August of 1891, mill agents in Lowell received a letter from the United Hebrew Charities inquiring whether Jews driven from their home countries by persecution could find work in the mills. The communication stated that "there are many skilled mechanics among their number—as well as families who have some experience and are well fitted to become operatives in mills and factories."² The mill towns of New England were viewed as desirable places to settle. The United Hebrew Charities attempted unsuccessfully to purchase a mill in Lowell. It was believed that Jews relocated away from ghettoes in urban centers would face less job competition as well as confront less anti-Semitism because their dispersal would insure less group visibility.

Still other Jews came directly to Lowell from Boston. Already an industrial town in the 1850s, in the brief span of two decades, Boston developed into the fourth largest city in the country. A port city, it became a center for Jewish immigration.³ Some Jews longed to leave the crowded city and move into rural areas where they hoped to find new entrepreneurial opportunities or ply their trades in unchartered waters.

The Jews in Lowell in the 1890s and early 1900s maintained someone at the Middlesex Street railroad depot to meet all trains. This person would speak in Yiddish to newcomers and aid them in finding lodgings and jobs. A network of support services was provided. Many came to Lowell consigned to relatives or wearing tags, sometimes inscribed with only the city's name, as a guide for ticket sellers and train conductors. Landstmanschaften associations (people from the same European regions) flourished and looked out for the newcomers. The support of people who had once had similar experiences helped cushion the transition from the old culture to the new. Some came to Lowell on recommendations of earlier immigrants from their European villages. After he or she had a job, the Jew sought to become Americanized. The greatest insult among Jews was to call a person a "greener" or "greenhorn." These new immigrants wanted desperately to become Americans.

In the late summer of 1873, the newspaper *Lowell Vox Populi* noted with approval the increasing numbers of Jews in Lowell. It singled out the B'nai Israel Society (founded in 1870) for the caliber of its members.⁴ It stated:

> Many members are engaged in trade, some are employed in workshops, others in professional and literary callings, and some in agricultural pursuits; and we are happy to know that they are doing well and many are numbered among our best citizens. In general they are

a quiet, intelligent and industrious class and add to this their natural taste for domestic life and they have a certain degree of independence, quietness of mind and a feeling of elevation tending to the promotion of pleasurable serenity, worth more than the largest wealth.[5]

By 1890 the view of Jews was changing. The local press reported:

Our Jew paupers are spreading typhus fever over the country. Those established by the Merrimack Manufacturing Company Agent Ludlam, appear to be in a fairly good condition, but further shipments of Russian Jews will have to be watched.

To offset this rumor, Agent Ludlam arranged for a tour of Jews at work in the Merrimack Manufacturing Company for a reporter who was immediately impressed and wrote:

The women are dark with lovely eyes and are not so Jewish in appearance as might be expected. They appear bright, willing in work and the mill managers say they make first class help. They were poverty stricken when they came here but are doing better now.[6]

The Jewish settlement flourished. Jews began to arrive in large numbers in the mill town along the Merrimack. Unlike some immigrant groups in Lowell, Jews never intended to go back to their countries of birth. They were setting down roots for life. They envisioned a permanent separation and put time and money into paying the ship passage for other family members. At first Jews lived in three-decker tenements. Jewish women often took in boarders to augment the meager resources of their families. By the 1890s, within the enclave of Hale and Howard Streets, there were kosher meat markets, fruit and vegetable stores, bakeries, synagogues, Hebrew schools, and even a ritual bath (mikvah). In his 1912 book, *Record of a City*, commemorating the 75th anniversary of Lowell, George Kenngott reports that the Hebrews can hardly be placed in the working class of Lowell and they seldom have more than one family in a tenement. As testimony to the vitality of the community, he enumerates that there were two Jewish newspapers, *Star of Bethlehem* and *Zion's Banner* and four synagogues.[7] Most Jews did not remain long in the mills. They were eager to become self-employed in order to avoid working on Saturday, the Sabbath. Jews were often told by mill supervisors, "if you don't come in on Saturday, don't come in Monday." Maurice Barlofsky reported that this was the experience of his father, Abraham, who came to Lowell in 1886 and went to work for the Merrimack Company. He was fired when he refused to work on Saturdays.[8]

As an alternative, some took to the roads as peddlers. Bennett Silverblatt, the first Jewish attorney in Lowell, recalled that his father, Samuel Silverblatt, who arrived in Lowell in the 1880s, set about peddling dry-goods from a pack on his back. As he observed: "The Jews were mostly peddlers—they sold everything off their backs. My father knew only a few words in English, though he spoke Russian, German, Polish, and Yiddish. If anyone asked him anything, he would say 'look in the basket.'"[9]

Esther Cohen, the daughter of Max Cohen, whose family was first to settle on Howard Street, recalled that her father was known as the junk man. "He and my brothers would leave early Monday every week with two horses pulling their wagon filled with pots and pans. They would be away until the Sabbath, sleeping at the homes of customers en route."[10]

Due to its small size, the community was never a hermetically contained ghetto as would have been found in Jewish areas of larger cities. It ranged in size from 200 families at the turn of the century to possibly 600 families later. A wide range of self help organizations developed. One of the first, even predating the establishment of formal synagogues, was the Israel Brotherhood Lodge, or five cent (fimph centaka) club—a burial society. Founded in 1893, members received a burial plot, a death benefit and medical care for a five-cent weekly charge. That same year, the first Jewish cemetery was established. Orthodox Jewish law requires quick burial, so a cemetery was sought nearby. However, Jews were refused land in Lowell, so five acres were purchased in Pelham, New Hampshire. This is an early example of religious discrimination—Jews could live in Lowell but could not be buried there. Having the cemetery so far away represented a hardship. Following Jewish tradition, burial was required within twenty-four hours of the death. The burial party had to travel by horse and wagon.

The first synagogue, Khilos Jacobe, the Congregation of Jacob, founded in 1897 at 8 McIntyre Street, was commonly referred to as The McIntyre Shul. Initially, members worshipped in a tenement flat. Its members were mostly of Austro-Hungarian origins. The Montefiore Synagogue, named after Sir Moses Montefiore, a British subject who was a benefactor of Jewish settlement in Palestine, was established in 1903 on Howard Street. Its members were mostly Polish, Russian and Lithuanian. Other smaller synagogues sprang up to accommodate the subtle variations in religious practices of the various national groups of Jews. The Russian Anshe Sfard broke away from the Montefiore and moved up Howard Street. In each synagogue, Yiddish was spoken a little differently. There was also the desire to have a synagogue that would remind them of their youth, for these Jews were still strangers in a strange land.

The community prospered in the early 20th century. Peddlers became store owners and some of their children became professionals. Some Jewish merchants branched out. The Rindler family ran a grocery store in the middle of the Polish Centralville neighborhood while another family operated a used jewelry store in the Little Canada neighborhood. First generation children, as did the generations that followed, went to the public schools. They attended the Abraham Lincoln Elementary School on the periphery of the Jewish settlement; in the afternoons they attended Hebrew schools sponsored by the synagogues. Most went on to Lowell High School (the first co-ed public high school in the U.S.).[11] Jewish parents supported the public schools as a way of insuring that their children would grow up American and mix with children from other groups. By contrast, some other ethnic groups such as the Irish, French, and Greeks established their own parochial schools. Jewish adults, especially the women, eager to become Americanized, attended evening classes at the Lincoln School or the International Institute where English language instruction was provided as well as preparation for citizenship.

Not all families could spare their children from work. Nathan Cohen, born in Russia in 1897, recalled that he came to Lowell in 1907 and went to work at age 15 as a floor sweeper at the Boott Mills. Nathan, an erudite man, was completely self-educated. While still a legal alien he was drafted into the U.S. Army in 1918 and sent to an army camp in Virginia. Upon his arrival, Nathan was told he could as an alien claim an exemption from the draft or choose to serve. He chose to serve and was to be sent overseas. On the eve of his departure, the World War I armistice was declared and a special federal court session was arranged to make on the spot citizens of the volunteer alien inductees. Nathan proudly recalled that the presiding judge, David Gardner Tyler, a grandson of President John Tyler, told the soldiers who were to be naturalized; "You are better citizens than I, I had to serve, you chose to serve."[12]

Upon his return to Lowell, Nathan started a small business making paper tubes. The business greatly expanded during World War II when it made paper tubes for artillery shells. He was preceded in Lowell by his father who resold grain bags picked up from local farmers. Nathan, who died in 1989 at the age of 92, had two sons; one became a rabbi, the other a physician.[13]

Three-decker tenements became two-deckers. Some of the more prosperous Jews became less orthodox and moved to single family homes in the middle-class lower Highlands area of Lowell on the outskirts of the original Jewish settlement. The impetus was the establishment in 1927 of Temple Beth El, the first conservative synagogue and combined community center, in the prestigious old Highland Club on Princeton Boulevard in the upper Highlands. It formerly had been used by mill owners, wealthy businessmen and other executives as a social club. In 1955 the old building was demolished and a new temple constructed there. Temple members built beautiful, substantial homes in the surrounding neighborhoods.

A small reform synagogue, Temple Emanuel, was established on West Forest Street in the upper Highlands in 1949. In 1969, the orthodox Montefiore Synagogue also started construction of a new synagogue in the upper Highlands on Westford Street to accommodate the majority of its members, who were by now gravitating to the outer edge of the upper Highlands. The closed Highland Congregational Church was demolished for the purpose of building this new orthodox synagogue. The dramatic residential shifts tied to synagogue renewals was poignantly symbolized in 1971 by a parade of members carrying the torahs from the old Montefiore Synagogue on Howard Street up Westford Street to the Highlands for the dedication of the new Montefiore Synagogue. This dispersion of the Jewish community away from the original kleine shtetl settlement left only the most pious elderly Jews on Howard Street. The area, no longer a center of Jewish activity, was torn down for urban renewal in the late 1960s.

World War II represented yet another turning point for many third generation children. After graduating from college, they never returned to Lowell, moving to surrounding communities or to the suburbs of greater Boston. For them occupations in the professions were common. These young people represented the embodiment of the American dream of expectation and fulfillment through hard work and achievement for their parents. The community's sights turned further away from the old Hale-Howard district where one could maintain orthodox traditions, such as walking to the synagogue on the Sabbath and easily upholding dietary restrictions.

In the 1970s there began a dramatic rebirth of the city of Lowell which had impact on the Jewish community as well. The establishment of Lowell National Historical Park, the growth of the high technology industry in the area, and the expanding University of Massachusetts Lowell campus, revitalized the city as a regional center for the entire Merrimack Valley. Jewish institutions also expanded. The community now supports a Hebrew day school, the Montefiore Synagogue, Temple Beth El and Willow Manor Nursing Home and Retirement Center, all of which provide a Jewish cultural atmosphere and a kosher kitchen—within a four-block area.

Descendents of original kleine shtetl families continue as active participants in these institutions and some have maintained dual membership in both the orthodox and the conservative synagogues. Their ties to the Jewish community often supersede ritual distinctiveness. For example, Nathan Cohen was simultaneously a president of the orthodox Montefiore Synagogue and a trustee of the conservative Temple Beth El. Contemporarily some women hold dual leadership positions in the synagogue and temple. Barbara Bernstein was president of Beth El Sisterhood while concurrently on the prasidium of Montefiore. The reform Congregation Shalom in the adjoining suburb of Chelmsford attracted Lowellians as well. Membership in Jewish organizations was re-energized by the infusion of Jewish high technology professionals and University of Massachusetts Lowell faculty who live in the area. However, in the 1990s, there has been an economic downturn in the region and today, membership in the synagogues remains static. In 1993, approximately half of the members of Temple Beth El were over sixty.[14] This reflects the fact that many young Jewish families prefer to settle in the surrounding towns of Chelmsford, Westford, Ayer, and Andover, where new synagogues have been established.

The original ethnic neighborhoods of Lowell surrounded the mill district. Each ethnic group—Irish, French, Greek, Polish, Jewish, and others—maintained territorial boundaries within which ethnic homogeneity generally prevailed.[15] Each had its own houses of worship, shops, and community structure, and were most often serviced by their own doctors, dentists, lawyers and pharmacists. Over time, some in each group moved up the economic ladder away from the central city area. Jews became securely entrenched in the desirable Highlands. Paradoxically, even though Jews prospered as entrepreneurs and some became millionaires and mill owners themselves, they did not attempt to move into the exclusive Belvidere district of the city where the Yankee establishment families had built their mansions high on the hill. The Belvidere neighborhood was long a bastion of Yankee Protestant control and a metaphor for success and assimilation at the highest socio-economic level of Lowell life.

After its incorporation in 1826, Lowell grew and developed rapidly. It was perceived as a city of opportunity and growth. From just one mill—the Merrimack—which began operation in 1823, there was a great mill expansion and a variety of supporting shops and businesses. The first decades after incorporation were viewed as Lowell's golden age. By 1840, Lowell was the second largest city in Massachusetts, with a population of 21,000. There was an economic downturn during the Civil War years (1861-65). Some mills ceased operation when the supply of cotton from the south was cut off. The economy again improved after 1870 into the eary 1900s. However, the city never again reached its prewar eminence as the major manufacturing center of the U.S. After the war, the Protestant mill women who had lost their jobs did not return. Their places were taken by a constant flow of new immigrants.

In the 1920s, the great mills began to fail or move south in search of cheaper non-union labor. Also it was no longer necessary to be near a water power source. Jews moved into this void by setting up marginal activities in some of the abandoned mills. Some rented floors of the mills to produce items such as mattresses, shoes and sweaters. In 1920, A. Paul Cohen established the Suffolk Knitting Company in the old Suffolk Mills. Still others used floors of the mills for warehousing cotton waste or wholesale supplies.

Notes

1. Howard Sachar, *The Course of Modern Jewish History* (New York: Dell Publishing Co., 1958) pp. 188-98.
2. Oscar Janowsky (ed.), *The American Jew* (New York: Jewish Publication Society, 1942) p. 152.
3. Isaac Fein, *Boston, Where it all Began* (Boston: Jewish Bicentennial Committee, 1976) p. 18.
4. This society predates any of the established synagogues and was charted for philanthropic, cultural and communal interests.
5. *American Israelite*, Volume 21, Oct. 3, 1873.
6. Cited in Frederick W. Coburn, *History of Lowell and its People* (New York: Lewis Historical Publishing, 1920) pp. 344-345. Note: A typhus epidemic had been taking place in Russia.
7. George Kenngott, *Record of a City* (New York: MacMillan, 1912) pp. 192-201.
8. Group interview with Jewish old timers, Willow Manor Nursing and Retirement Center, Shirley Kolack, Mark Levine, June 2, 1988.
9. *Lowell Sunday Sun*, "A Native Recalls Old City," June 13, 1971.
10. Interview with Esther Cohen, Willow Manor Nursing and Retirement Center, Mark Levine, 1987.
11. Jill Parker, "Changing Times: A Century and a Half at Lowell High School." Brochure on Exhibit, Lowell: Patrick J. Morgan Cultural Center, 1990. Note: Lowell High opened in 1831.
12. Oral History Interview with Nathan Cohen, Center for Lowell History, July 7, 1985, and group interview, Shirley Kolack, Mark Levine, 1988.
13. Interview, Nathan Cohen, 1988.
14. Temple Beth El, Report of Survey of Membership (Unpublished), 1994.
15. Margaret Terrell Parker, Lowell, *A Study of Industrial Development* (New York: MacMillan, 1940) pp. 89-91.

Chapter 3
ORGANIZATIONS

Paralleling the cultural shock that the Eastern European Jews experienced upon arriving in the city was their collective efforts to establish an organized Jewish life to solidify and maintain their group cohesion. They had been uprooted and were seeking affiliations that would bring them security and a sense of belonging. Foundations were laid for a network of social welfare and religious organizations that would aid economic survival as well as provide cultural and religious continuity. As with the other immigrant groups, a great part of life from birth to death was spent within the institutional framework of one's own group.

The earliest organizations were religious in nature. In the practice of their religion, Jews found refuge from anti-Semitism and a bulwark against assimilation. Judaism provided them with a way of life in a new and often hostile environment. There was a proliferation of small synagogues, each catering to Jews of a particular national origin—Russian, Lithuanian, Polish, Austro-Hungarian. All were strictly orthodox and their members were Yiddish-speaking. The McIntyre Synagogue, organized in 1897, was the first synagogue to have an official rabbi. He was Elias Wolfson, who also ran a kosher butcher shop. A butcher was a respected, pious man with a knowledge of correct ritual slaughter; he set standards for the community. The most revered religious leader, a man still spoken of with awe, was Rabbi Joseph Warren, who officiated at Temple Beth El from 1930 until his death in 1966. He presided over the development of this conservative synagogue as it outgrew its space in the old Highland Club and gave impetus to the building of a beautiful new synagogue to accommodate its large membership. During Rabbi Warren's tenure it became, and remains today, the most important Jewish institution in the city with an active sisterhood and brotherhood. With the completion of Temple Beth El's new building in 1955, there was in place both a modern synagogue and an expanded community center. The new temple center provided a highly adequate meeting place for various religious and secular Jewish organizations, including a variety of youth groups. The synagogue was a gathering place where one could maintain common bonds with other Jews on many different levels. How farsighted Temple Beth El had been in establishing a combined synagogue and community center is expressed in the following excerpt from the greetings by Rabbi Harry Levi of Temple Israel, Boston, which appeared in the 1927 Lowell Community Center Dedication Booklet.

> I am especially glad that the building is to serve as a rallying place for every kind of communal Jewish activity. Jewish centers are being built all over the country because they respond to a real Jewish need. And wherever they have been built they have immediately succeeded. Here Jewish organizations meet and take counsel. Here the community comes to consider its common problems. Here young men and women come to study and to play. Here children come to study religion and to be helped by those in charge to a better way of life. Here all who enter find moral and spiritual and even physical direction and uplift.
>
> I like the intimate connection between religion and all the activities for which the average center stands. Religion is life and must touch its every expression or it is a failure. And all our Jewish interests must be linked up with our faith or they lack direction, inspiration, and consecration. Religion is worship translated into life. It is life springing from worship.

Montefiore Synagogue, which has maintained its adherence to traditional orthodox Judaism, dedicated its new building in the upper Highlands in 1971. It pioneered in Jewish education by sponsoring the Merrimack Valley Hebrew Academy, a Hebrew day school, where both secular and religious subjects are taught through the sixth grade. The school was founded in 1970 under the guidance of Rabbi Abraham Witty, who served as rabbi, principal, and teacher. Today the school, although independent, is still housed on the synagogue grounds. Its students are drawn from the surrounding communities and as far away as New Hampshire. A large number of the seventy children who attend are from non-orthodox families. Traditionally, education has been for Jews a primary means of shaping their identity. As in the country as a whole, a sizeable number of young Jewish families in Lowell have returned to orthodox practices. At the same time, there is a reaching out to the general community. In an ecumenical spirit, both the rabbis of Temple Beth El and Montefiore are members of an umbrella interfaith organization of clergymen in Lowell. Member priests, rabbis, and ministers sponsor a weekly radio program—"Faith Alive".

A small reform synagogue, Temple Emanuel, was established in the Highlands in 1949. Its first rabbi was Rabbi Alvin Reeves. The congregation's members come from surrounding areas as well as Lowell itself. Some of its original members belonged to Temple Beth El and separated from it based on a desire for changes in the religious services, which were to include a choir accompanied by an organ. This synagogue embraces a liberal ideology of adapting religious practices to modern times. Its present rabbi, Everett Gintler, has a following beyond the Merrimack Valley region.

Even before 1890, there were Jewish fraternal organizations to provide services that the Jewish community required for survival. Burial societies were crucial. To be among the volunteers who prepared the bodies of the dead for burial was looked upon as a high honor. They had their own associations (Chevra Kadisha) and, upon their deaths, a special section of the Jewish cemetery in Pelham, New Hampshire, was set aside for their burial. Although the Chevra Kadisha charged for their services, all money received was donated to charity. According to orthodox custom from the moment of death until internment a Chevra Kadisha member would sit with the deceased and read scripture.

In 1975 the Pelham cemetery was turned over to the Montefiore Synagogue. In addition to it, another Jewish cemetery in Chelmsford, Massachusetts, was established in 1913 by the Independent Lodge of Brith Abraham. In 1944, when its members numbered only a few, the cemetery was sold to Temple Beth El. Burial societies were considered a most important organizational structure. Educational organizations could wait but everyone would need a burial plot. Each new Jew who arrived in the city was listed in the records of the various burial groups so plots would be available.

Other organizations, such as the Ladies Hebrew Helping Hand Society (references relating to it appear as early as 1873)[1] and the Gemiluth Chassodim (kind acts) Society, performed acts of charity for destitute Jews in need of money for coal, rent, food and clothing. Dedicated women were the volunteers for these long-enduring organizations (both existed into the 1970s). The Ladies Helping Hand Society's yearly dues were three dollars, which could be paid in installments. Monthly meetings were held at Talmud Torah Hall on Howard Street in the heart of the Jewish district. All aid was given anonymously and the recipients' names were never revealed. To raise money for its various charities, the Society held an annual Ladies Ball. In a continuation of these social service traditions throughout the 1970s, Jewish women made monthly visits to Tewksbury State Hospital where they put on skits for patients. An educational component to organizational life was always apparent. The Lowell Hebrew Independent Club was chartered on July 24, 1887, with the mission of instructing its members in the English language and in the duties of American citizenship and the assistance of such as are needy."[2]

An important motivation for maintaining a network of self-help organizations was the belief that Jews should help their own. For centuries Jews had faced persecution in European ghettoes; this created among them a collective ethic of responsibility for each other. Over time there was a transformation from organizations with only a religious focus to quasi-secularized ones. Jews rejected the politically-connected charity available through city hall. Old timers state with pride that the organizational structures they maintained allowed all Jews to avoid the need for public assistance. It was accepted that to the community in which a man has prospered, he owes a return.

Because these first arrivals spoke only Yiddish and had no credit, it was impossible for them to receive bank loans. Therefore, Hebrew Free Loan Societies were established to aid those immigrants who wished to start businesses or pay for housing. The money borrowed was paid back monthly in amounts that the recipients could afford. In the 1900s, three credit unions were formally charted in Lowell by the state of Massachusetts. The Ideal Credit Union was formed in 1910. By 1926 there was also the Highland Credit Union and the Lowell Credit Union. Prominent Jews in the community were signers of these charters. These credit unions provided a lending network. Credit was extended based on one's word, character and good name. A handshake most often was sufficient to seal the deal.

Social welfare programs for Lowell Jews generally were affiliated with synagogues or Landsmanschaften organizations (people from the same region in the "old country"). An exception was the Arbeiter Ring (Workmen's Circle) established nationally in 1900 to bring together immigrant Jewish workers of a socialist persuasion who identified with a secular Jewish culture as an alternative to religious involvement.[3] It promoted social reform for workers, a socialist labor educational program, Yiddish studies, and other cultural activities, as well as providing insurance, health, and burial benefits. The Lowell chapter never acquired a large membership, as was the case in the neighboring mill towns of Lawrence and Haverhill, in part because Lowell Jews saw themselves as capitalist-businessmen rather than workers. It is ironic that this perception by many Jews prevailed in a city that was designed with the overall economic goal of maintaining control over workers through a form of corporate paternalism.

Some organizations sponsored nationally by the earlier established German Jews also formed in Lowell. For the German Jews who were thoroughly assimilated, Judaism was more a religious faith than an encompassing way of life. Their goal was to Americanize the East European Jews whom they saw as "greenhorns." They wanted the Yiddish speaking immigrants to abandon their old world cultural and religious practices and rapidly become transformed.

The first organization to affect all immigrants was the German-Jewish sponsored Hebrew Immigrant Aid Association (HIAS) that helped with the daunting task of settling the new arrivals. HIAS located family members and arranged for jobs and places to live. Another organization supported by German Jews was the Educational Alliance; it provided educational programs for children and adults. It was a combination of night school, settlement house, gymnasium, and public forum. Among its affiliates was the Young Men's and Young Women's Hebrew Associations. Their overall mission was to Americanize the "vulgar" immigrants. Slowly the Alliance began to acknowledge that the East Europeans had brought with them a vibrant culture that should not simply be repressed, and that assimilation had to be viewed as a process in which a balance was maintained between past and present. There were always passionate debates within the organization over whether it should stress traditional Hebraic and Yiddish or American culture and customs. Today, as in the past, new immigrants of all groups still experience conflict over whether to maintain traditional ways or make a clean sweep into the "American way of life."

Fraternal organizations that combined social, educational, and service functions flourished during the 1920s and 1930s. The Benjamin S. Pouzzner Lodge of B'nai B'rith, founded in 1925, was named in honor of its first president, Benjamin Pouzzner, who died in 1926 at the age of forty-two. Pouzzner was the dynamic editor and owner of the *Lowell Sunday Telegram News*. This paper was later sold by Pouzzner's widow to the *Lowell Sun*. At his untimely death, Pouzzner was slated to become the District President of B'nai B'rith. The local lodge also had active youth components such as the B'nai B'rith Youth Organization (BBYO) and Aleph Zadek Aleph (AZA). B'nai B'rith played a vibrant role in the community, sponsoring many events such as father-son nights, speakers on Jewish themes and support for Jewish causes worldwide. Many elders recall with satisfaction the recognition the Lowell Lodge received for its model performance; its leaders were sent as a team to install the officers of lodges throughout Massachusetts.

A national spotlight was focused on Lowell during the years 1947 through 1953, when Frank Goldman, a prominent local lawyer, presided as the International President of B'nai B'rith. During his tenure in office, Goldman met with many world leaders, among them Presidents Truman and Eisenhower, and the Prime Minister of Israel, David Ben-Gurion. He played a role in President Truman's decision to recognize the state of

Israel. An account of Goldman's dramatic behind-the-scenes activities leading up to this historic event is recounted in *Genesis 1948* by Daniel Kurzman.[4] In the book, Kurzman tells of Frank Goldman's strategic actions to convince President Truman to support the creation of the state of Israel. Goldman involved Eddie Jacobson, Truman's old pal and business partner, in reversing the President's position of non-support to a position of full support of the state of Israel through the action of the United Nations.

The Jewish community was too small for the simultaneous functioning of similar organizations. Organizations cooperated and jointly provided building blocks for Jewish survival. In 1927, Temple Beth El combined its sisterhood with the Lowell chapter of Hadassah, a national organization for women that focused on Palestine and the needs of European Jews. Talented local women presented book reviews and poetry readings as part of year-long cultural and educational programs. A collection of verses, "City Poems" by Rose Goldman, was printed in "Alentour," in 1936.

There were successful fundraising events for Jewish causes both international and local. In 1936, the year of the devastating flood in Lowell, money that had been raised to buy a grand piano was given instead to aid the flood victims. Initially, the women met in the intimate settings in their homes but, when attendance greatly increased at these popular events, they moved to the old Marlborough Hotel. A prime reason for the eventual purchase in 1927 of the Highland Club was to establish the Lowell Jewish Community Center where both men's and women's groups could meet. Recognition of the importance of the women to community life occurred in 1934 when they were invited by the men to appoint three members annually as Trustees of the Community Center. The first women appointees brought a contribution of $1000 to their first meeting.[5]

Programs for youth also were supported by joint sisterhood/Haddassah endeavors. Two of the most popular were the Hadassah Buds and a sisterhood-sponsored Girl Scout troop. The social life of preteen and teenage girls revolved around the activities of these groups. A charter member of the Buds recalled that the organization was established in the early 1920s with annual dues of ten cents and a yearly budget of ten dollars. She vividly remembered that the girls, dressed in white with Jewish National Fund imprinted on blue bands across their chests, trudged to every Jewish home to collect the usual donation of ten cents. In 1933, at the peak of the Great Depression years, the sisterhood waived the registration fee of fifty cents for indigent members of its Girl Scout troop.

In the 1920s Temple Beth El sponsored Boy Scout and Girl Scout troops; both remained popular throughout the years. The boys were led by members of the Jewish War Veterans. There was also a variety of other youth organizations that served to keep young people actively involved in their Jewish heritage. A club for Bar Mitzvahed boys kept alive the meaningful experience they all had shared. A Young Men's Hebrew Association (YMHA) and a Young Women's Hebrew Association (YWHA) were also active as well as a Community Center Players dramatic group. Junior Hadassah was formed as a link to unite young unmarried Jewish women with the senior parent organization. It provided a meeting ground for social contacts and an opportunity for young women to raise money for Jews in Palestine with projects of their own. Each year they had an annual musical event. Junior Hadassah was reported to be the most active organization in town.

The mission of some organizations was to keep spirits up and bodies healthy. Most fondly remembered is the Morgan (sic) David baseball team. The young men (ages 16-19) wore uniforms bearing the Star of David. To play baseball was to be American. Their rabbi pointed out that the spelling on their uniforms was incorrect and should have been Mogan David, but it was too late. The uniforms already had been purchased (see photo circa 1925, page 88). Once a year the Mogan Davids put on a show and sponsored a dance at the Rex Ballroom. The program for the 1935 gala was entitled "Second Edition of Men in Gowns," followed by dancing until 1 a.m.; subscription was 75 cents. True to the Jewish tradition in Lowell of providing a learning dimension in all organizations, the Mogan Davids held a series of debates in which members took opposing views on topical current events. Benjamin Sandler, a retired lawyer who was an active participant in these activities, attributed the esprit de corps generated by the group's members to their restricted physical mobility due to a lack of cars.

Of necessity, the local community was the centerpiece of youth activity.[6]

The Tenth Anniversary Commemorative Booklet of the Lowell Hebrew Center (1927-1937) highlights the myriad of activities of the numerous Jewish organizations. It states: "No Jew in Lowell need feel alone. However old, however young, one may be, there is some organization at the Center to which one can be linked." This decade truly represented a period of the flowering of religious and cultural activity. Social and religious lives were intertwined.

World War I and World War II were turning points for Jewish participation in the wider Lowell community. Jews were enthusiastic and patriotic participants in these wars. In both wars, they were well represented in the fighting forces overseas and in community efforts on the homefront. On the eve of World War I, David Van Greenby, a local Jewish realtor, founded a chapter of the Jewish War Veterans. His son Donald, who served in the infantry in World War II, remains the driving force behind this still-active organization.

In May, 1915, three young men who were members of the Young Men's Hebrew Association in Lowell (YMHA) set out on foot for the Pan American Exposition in San Francisco to publicize the activities of their organization and to interconnect with YMHA's in cities along the way. World War I had begun and they wore boy scout outfits modeled after soldiers' uniforms. The mayor of Lowell saw them off and then-Governor Walsh provided a letter of introduction. En route, the boys gave patriotic speeches and sang songs. Their journey was not completed because one of the walkers, Max Greenberg, became ill in Detroit. He kept a diary and scrapbook of these events.[7] This undertaking represented a reaching out to a world beyond Lowell.

Although the United States entered the Second World War only after the Japanese attack on Pearl Harbor in December, 1941, the Jews of Lowell were deeply concerned earlier and involved with opposing fascism. They were mindful of the need to aid the thousands of Jewish refugees who in 1939, fleeing Germany and Austria, sought asylum in the U.S. At the peak of this resettlement, 36 Jewish refugees were housed and cared for in Lowell. Affidavits were signed to guarantee that they would never become public charges. The Jewish community was prepared to underwrite any expenses that might occur. These new immigrants made rapid adjustments to American life and almost all of them eventually migrated to larger urban centers.[8]

Some Lowellian Jews had relatives who died at the hands of the Nazis. The tragedy of the Nazi holocaust, which resulted in the mass murder of six million European Jews, was a crucial motivating force for them to become strong supporters of the founding of the state of Israel. Lowell Jews joined with Zionist organizations throughout the country to build a climate favorable to the establishment of a Jewish homeland. They lavished money and support of refugees both during and after the war. In the post-war years funds were raised through the Lowell United Jewish Appeal for the relief of survivors of the concentration camps. For Jews then and now, significant defining events for their shared identity are the Holocaust and the establishment of Israel.

During World War II the Jewish community acted as an extended family for the needs of the Jewish personnel at nearby Fort Devens. Rabbi Warren of Temple Beth El served as their civilian Jewish chaplain. Local Jewish organizations jointly sponsored social events such as bagel breakfasts for soldiers at the local United Service Organization (USO) and parties for soldiers at the Lowell General Hospital division at Fort Devens. A fighter plane was named in honor of Temple Beth El's Sisterhood and Haddasah for successfully selling $110,000 in U.S. savings bonds. The B'nai B'rith lodge collected substantial donations to provide recreational facilities for non-sectarian use on board ships and at army posts. The Jewish Community Center compiled detailed war records of the young Jewish men who entered military service; included were accounts of those wounded in action or decorated for bravery.[9]

The Second World War, followed by the post war period, represented a watershed for Jews in broadening their interests and cooperation in non-sectarian causes. They were enthusiastic participants in the war-related activities of the American Red Cross, including its fundraising. Prominent Jews were members of the Lowell Board of the Selective Service. William Levine, a founder of Towers Motor Parts Corporation, became its head. Morris Palefsky, a builder, was chairman of

Civil Defense. A. Paul Cohen, President of the Suffolk Knitting Mills, which manufactured sweaters for soldiers, was elected President of the National Knitted Outerwear Association in 1943. Cohen served as chairman of this industry's advisory committee to the Office of Price Administration and was a member of the War Production Board.

Jewish men became active in local business and service associations. William Cantor, a Vice President of the family-owned Cantor Insurance Company, held office in the Lowell Rotary Club. He was also chairman of the Lowell United Fund. William Levine was president of the Lion's Club. Maurice Barlofsky, a lawyer, became a director of a local bank. By the end of the war, the exclusive social clubs, including the now-defunct Yorick and the Vesper Country Club (established in 1870), that long had barred their doors to Jews, began to admit them.

The war represented for all ethnic groups a shared goal of uniting for survival and lessened the impact of narrow parochial concerns. A repeated theme was the ideal that we are all Americans and must unite. A hightened acceptance of cultural pluralism and tolerance of group distinctiveness was a legacy of World War 11.[10] Even though physically and socially separated, the various ethnic groups were able to put aside their own special agendas and join together. Wartime behavior was an example of the sociological principle that people generally will put common interests above their own selfish interests only when there is a threat to their existence.

Always small in number, Jews were not significant in city politics. In Lowell, each ethnic group tended to vote as a block, and it was the Irish with their large numbers who, by the late 19th century, had taken over political control from the Yankee elite. By 1882, the majority of the Board of Aldermen and the mayor of Lowell were Irish.[11] For the first three decades of the 20th century, Jews voted for Republican candidates, nationally and locally. They supported the party that represented business interests with which Jews identified. The French were highly skilled workers and small businessmen who also voted for Republicans. Democratic patronage typically went to the Irish and the other large working-class groups who joined the Irish in voting for Democrats.

A shift in voting patterns for Jews occurred when Franklin Delano Roosevelt was swept into office during the depression years of the 1930s. Jews as champions of help for those in need overwhelmingly approved the humanistic New Deal social welfare programs put into place by Roosevelt. Jews had a fervor for social justice related to their historical battle with hostile authorities. They continued, however, to support the conservative Republican congresswoman, Edith Nourse Rogers, the daughter and heir of the patrician family owners of the Boott Mills. On the eve of World War II, Rogers introduced significant Jewish refugee legislation in Congress and was an advocate for the state of Israel. She served in Congress during the years 1925 through 1960.

At the end of the war, there was an exodus of third-generation, college-educated young people to suburbs in the greater Boston area. Trained as professionals, with horizons lifted by their college experiences, they set their sights beyond Lowell. Many had attended Ivy League colleges, some through the government sponsored educational G.I. Bill. They were eager to venture beyond the boundaries of what they now viewed as a small town. They could make life choices that had been unavailable to their parents' generation.

These young adults, educated in the public schools of Lowell, had also attended after-school Hebrew classes and been actively involved in synagogue youth organizations. Talmud Torahs (Hebrew schools) that met in the afternoons were a way of keeping Jewish culture alive without interfering with the public school curriculum or disturbing the acculturation process as would have been the case if Jewish children had attended full-time Jewish parochial schools. They were poised to accomplish their parents' expectations of fulfilling the American dream of high achievement and material rewards through discipline, hard work, and education.

The stress on learning that was apparent throughout most of the Jewish religious and secular, organizations, served the community well. In 1910, the Hebrew Free School was founded by Gabriel Kahn to provide instruction for bar mitzvah boys. In addition, many elders of the community gave private Hebrew lessons. Until recently, there was a social group that met once a month, whose sole purpose was to keep the Yiddish language alive.

Jews in Lowell, as in other small towns, experienced isolation and a feeling of separateness more so than the multitudes of Jews concentrated in larger cities.[12] This fueled a strong desire for them to cling together and keep alive their Jewish identity. Often the community behaved as one large extended family. Ida Levy recalled that during the early years, all the women would cook and prepare for the bris (ritual circumcision of the eight day old male), and, if a woman's husband died, all the neighbors would contribute and help take care of her. When there was a simcha (celebration), everyone rejoiced, and when there was a tragedy, everyone mourned.[13] The network of organizations they developed allowed them to maintain their traditions and, at the same time, provide the security needed to venture into relationships with non-Jews in secular causes in the wider community.

By contrast, Jews in large urban centers, while also in a minority position, had a visibly significant ethnic presence. They had greater resources than small town Jews and could provide for their members a variety of religious and communal services.[14]

Like the other immigrant groups in Lowell, Jews sustained voluntary institutions to further their collective goals and also for the simple human pleasure of forming a smaller world within a larger impersonal society. Participation in organizational life provided the building blocks for survival, served as a training ground for leadership and set the stage for upward mobility. The self-help organizational framework paved the way for generating substantial upper middle and professional classes most dramatically mirrored in the shifts over the generations in occupational status. In spite of setbacks over the years, such as during the period of the great depression, Jews from humble beginnings prospered and their children became college educated.

Notes

1. *American Israelite*, Vol. 21, Oct. 3, 1873. (references to Ladies Helping Hand appear).
2. Massachusetts State Archives. Certificate of Organizations, Vol. 141, p. 109.
3. Irving Howe, *World of Our Fathers* (New York: Harcourt, Brace, Jovanovich, Inc., 1976) p. 358.
4. Daniel Kurzman, *Genesis :1948* (New York: World Publishing Co., 1970) pp. 120-124.
5. Hadassah and Sisterhood of Temple Beth El, *An Adventure in Lowell Jewish Communal Life 1923-1948*, Silver Anniversary Issue: December 9, 1948.
6. Interview with Benjamin Sandler, Shirley Kolack, 1989.
7. Max Greenberg, Diary, 1915.
8. Rabbi Joseph Warren, Unpublished report. History of the Lowell Hebrew Community Center & Temple Beth El, 1939-1955.
9. Rabbi Joseph Warren, Report.
10. Marc Scott Miller, *The Irony of Victory: World War II and Lowell, Massachusetts* (Chicago: University of Illinois Press, 1988) pp. 102-103.
11. Mary Blewett, "The Mills and the Multitudes: A Political History," in *Cotton Was King*, Arthur Eno, Jr., ed. (New Hampshire Publishing Company, in collaborations with The Lowell Historical Society, 1976) p. 174.
12. Sheva Medjuck, "Jewish Survival in Small Communities in Canada," *The Jews in Canada*, Robert Brym, William Shaffer and Morton Weinfelds, eds. (Toronto: Oxford University Press, 1993) pp. 363-375.
13. Interview with Ida Levy, Sandra Palefsky, "Origins of the Jewish Community of Lowell," Unpublished paper, 1982.
14. Medjuck, p. 366.

Chapter 4

OCCUPATIONAL PATTERNS

Occupational status is the single most defining aspect of a person's position in American society. How one makes a living is a measure of educational background, lifestyle, and values. It is an important objective indicator of social class. Jews understood this well. Wherever the Jews of Eastern Europe settled they displayed a strong determination to depart quickly from their working class status and become self-employed.[1] They passionately desired to have their children educated and become professionals. Jews arriving with little money and few skills achieved remarkable economic success. Nowhere was this movement upward for an entire group more dramatic than in Lowell. As for other immigrants, the initial impetus for coming to Lowell was the availability of unskilled manual work in the mills. For Jews however, a variety of factors intervened to make their employment in the mills short lived.

Conditions in the mills proved unsuitable for pious Jews and interfered with the practice of their religious rituals. Conflict over the Saturday Sabbath observance was often the breaking point. European Jews, long historic victims of arbitrary anti-Semitism, desired to be responsible and independent. They yearned to become self employed merchants and thus avoid discriminatory situations. They wanted to compete on the basis of their own merit and not be dependent on the good will of those in charge who might happen to dislike Jews.[2]

The immediate alternative to mill work was to return to the work roles that traditionally had been available to impoverished European Jews—that of rag pickers, junk dealers, and peddlers. At first, with packs on their backs, later with horse drawn carts, they combed the countryside selling and collecting bottles, pans, rags, and scrap metal. Jews also sold recycled wares to the immigrant mill workers, just as they had formerly done to European peasants. As fortunes improved, they began to sell from push carts and in small family-operated stores in the Hale-Howard Jewish section where they also provided for the needs of other Jews.

Dietary restrictions required kosher butcher shops, bakeries, and delicatessens. Kosher food is ritually fit according to Jewish law. Fruit and vegetable stands, as well as a variety of clothing establishments, abounded. Cobblers and tailors plied their trades. There was even a privately owned mikva, a bath house for ritual bathing. Thus the heart of the Jewish area was a vibrant center—a Kleine Shtetl (a small village) with a warren of Jewish owned stores throbbing with activities and providing goods and services for the entire community. Jews, as other ethnic groups, first began their move up the social class ladder by catering to the needs of their own group. An ethnic community that is largely segregated provides a captive market for an emerging middle class of professionals and shopkeepers.[3]

Over time there was a progression from peddler to small store owner to a shop on "main street." Many Jewish-owned stores expanded and moved into the downtown shopping area where they became familiar landmarks. Among them were several men's and women's clothing stores: Bass's Cloak and Suit Company and Newman's Clothing on Central Street; Lemkin's Women's Apparel on Merrimack Street. In 1898 Morris Lemkin, a Russian immigrant, came from Boston to Lowell and opened a small women's store. Over the years the business thrived. Herman Lemkin, who still lives in Lowell, recalls that as a teenager, his job was to trim the store windows. He proudly states that the window displays were on a par with big city stores. Herman especially enjoyed accompanying his father on buying sprees to New York to select new merchandise. When his father died in 1940, Herman took over the store. The business greatly expanded and additional floor space was incorporated from adjacent stores. An innovation established in the 1950s was to have twice-weekly fashion shows at the

Strand Theater where large crowds came to get a peek at the latest styles and see a double feature for 99 cents.[4]

The store closed its doors in 1986 after operating continuously for 89 years. Lemkin contributes its success to an appeal to women with a flair for fashion and the personal services provided for customers. His two sons, one an accountant and the other in real estate, were not interested in the business, a fact that is hard for Herman to understand. He said, "I loved the fashion business. It was like being in show business."[5]

Grey's Furniture Company was also on Central Street. Miriam Chosiod recalled that her father came to Lowell from New York in 1903 to work in the furniture business of his uncle. At first they worked from a horse drawn cart, later establishing Grey's Furniture Store.[6] Often entire families worked in the stores. Wives would often serve as clerks and were reported to know as much about these small businesses as their husbands. Some were extended family operations. Brothers often were partners; a cousin might serve as bookkeeper. At some point relatives often left to branch out on their own. There were great varieties of independent stores—jewelry, haberdashery, hardware, five-and-dime, pharmacies, and used clothing. Quite often, when a man saved a few dollars, he opened a second-hand store. Enterprising women rented out rooms and took in boarders. Religious bonds were strong. All Jewish merchants closed their stores on the Jewish high holidays: Rosh Hashanah (the Jewish New Year) and Yom Kipper (the Day of Atonement).

Overall there were two kinds of business ventures: traditional spinoffs from peddling, or marginal new endeavors where there would be little competition and renewed opportunity. The burgeoning entertainment field was also an attraction. As early as 1909, movies were shown in Lowell. From the 1920s to the 1960s downtown Lowell was a major mecca for the Merrimack Valley and movies were what people flocked to town to see.[7] Sam Knopf owned and operated the Colonial Theater, Norman Glassman owned and operated the Rialto, the Capitol, and the Victory Tower Memorial Palace theaters. All were popular movie houses. Nat Silver, who managed the Strand Theater during World War II, is remembered for bringing film stars to Lowell for war bond promotions. During the depression years of the 1930s, Joseph Solomont and his brothers, Meyer and Sy, became the proprietors of the Blue Room Nightclub and Restaurant. They also booked performers such as Cab Callaway into the Lowell Memorial Auditorium. The Solomont brothers later were pioneers in long-term nursing home care. The family-owned Willow Manor Retirement Center in Lowell is a model institution for care of the elderly. The sons of Joseph Solomont carry on this tradition. Alan, as President and chief executive, along with David, Jay, and Ahron, are joint owners of ADS, a management and consulting firm in Andover, Massachusetts, considered a premier provider of innovative practices for care of the elderly. The firm manages 32 nursing homes and is also developing assisted living projects that offer seniors apartment-style living with housekeeping and health care. In a recent *Boston Globe* article on emerging businesses, ADS was highly touted for mixing progressive social values and business acumen.[8] Alan who in 1977 received a nursing degree from the University of Lowell, later became the chairman of the University's Board of Trustees.

Benjamin Pouzzner, first a newspaper distributor, later became the editor and owner of the *Lowell Sunday Telegram*. Other Jews bought real estate. They began by acquiring ownership of housing in the Jewish area. By 1910, most of the buildings in the Jewish section were Jewish owned. Those who remained workers went into skilled trades. Carpenters and roofers became builders and contractors. Morris Palefsky, a self-taught builder, constructed the first apartment house in Lowell. Morris Gardens still stands on Westford and Pine Streets in the Highlands area. Esrael Greenberg was also an early builder of single family houses in Lowell. His grandson, Donald Van Greenby, is today the owner of a Lowell real estate agency.

Later, some Jews took over ownership of declining or abandoned mills. A city geared to 19th century needs, Lowell found its textile mills could not satisfactorily compete in the 20th century. In the 1940s, David Ziskind and his son, Jacob, bought the Merrimack Manufacturing Company, the first and largest of the great mills. The family owned and operated the mill until it closed in 1956.[9] The estate of Jacob Ziskind largely supplied the funds for the building of the present-day Temple Beth El. Starting in the 1950s, Joan Fabric was owned and operated by the Ansin family—father, Harold, and sons, Lawrence and

Joseph. It was the last remaining Jewish-owned textile manufacturing company, growing from a medium sized manufacturer of furniture fabrics into one of the largest producers of automotive fabrics in the U.S. In 1988, the Ansins sold the company, which remains in operation today.

A prominent ongoing family-owned service business is the Cantor Insurance Company, founded in 1921 by Jacob Cantor, a first generation Russian immigrant. He started as a debit life insurance collector for one of the national insurance companies. He would go door-to-door in the Jewish settlement collecting weekly payments for life insurance policies. The company expanded and prospered under the management of Jacob's sons, William and James, both among the first Jewish graduates of Ivy League colleges (Harvard and Brown) and is now third generation family-run. It currently represents some of the most prestigious nationwide insurance companies.

By 1920, there were very few Jews who still worked in the declining mills. Most Jews were self-employed merchants. After World War II, Jewish-owned stores began to close; some were taken over by chain stores, others folded because college-educated sons of the 1940s did not want to manage the family-run shops of their immigrant fathers. They were no longer interested in small business ventures as their parents had been. American-born Jewish college graduates of the 1920s, the sons and daughters of the early settlers, had been content to join in family enterprises or to practice law and medicine in Lowell.[10] By contrast the later generation preferred to practice the professions for which they had been trained in large urban centers, as well as seek new career opportunities. The final death knell for the old downtown stores was the burgeoning growth of shopping malls along nearby highways.

Collectively, Jews rose as a class and prospered, but there were exceptions. Sidney Muskovitz, born in 1918 in Lowell, was a son of Russian born Jewish parents. His father, a tinsmith, became a peddler; his mother worked in a mill. At the age of nineteen Sidney began work in the dye house of the Merrimack Mill. He recounted that when he married he got a job as machine oiler, which was considered more desirable because he earned five cents more an hour than other workers, raising his hourly rate to 45 cents. He worked as an oiler for thirty years until forced to retire because of bad health. He notes that the job was dirty, hot, noisy, miserable, and dangerous, but there were no better jobs. He oiled and wiped hundred of oil holes in the carding machines where his hands could get caught between belts, pulleys, and gears.[11]

There were lost opportunities and unfulfilled dreams for some due to discrimination. There was never organized anti-Semitism against Jews, possibly because they were so small in number. However, individuals who sought employment in the public sector throughout the pre-World War II years, in city hall, or the utilities such as the Lowell Electric, Telephone or Gas companies, and even in professions such as teaching, were turned away. Benjamin Sandler, a retired lawyer, recalled that his sister, upon graduating from Lowell Normal School, could not obtain a position as a teacher because of discriminatory practices by the Lowell School Department. Therefore, she reluctantly abandoned the profession for which she qualified and became a secretary.[12] There is no record of any Jews having been elected to any city office. Voters in Lowell tended to vote along ethnic lines. Jews were never more than two percent of the population. A significant event occurred when Reuben Rosenguard was hired after World War II by city hall to work in the Assessor's office. It was not until the 1950s that Jews were appointed to positions to develop and implement governmental programs in Lowell. Fanny Moore, whose father had emigrated to Lowell from Kiev in the Ukraine, was hired under Title I to teach English as a second language in the public schools, and Dr. Max Hyman was made a consultant for the Model Cities project.[13]

Growth in the entire Greater Merrimack Valley region in the 1970s led to an infusion of Jews into the area. There are now almost 10,000 Jews in the valley, with approximately 2,000 of them living in the Greater Lowell area.[14] Many are employed as engineers and managers in the high technology firms that dot the area, such as Wang Laboratories, Digital, and Mitre. A sizable number are employees of the University of Massachusetts Lowell as professors and researchers. Twenty-five to thirty Jewish doctors are on the staff of the hospitals in Lowell. There are older, prosperous Jews who remain and some second and third generation family businesses still are in operation, such as Melvin and Libby Glazer's Parrot Hat, Joseph Ferman's Draperies Design, Jerry Porton's Middlesex Paper Tube, and Garnick's T.V. and Stereo, jointly owned by Robert, Paul and David, three brothers and Sylvia, their mother. Melvin Glazer states that Parrot Hat is doing well because "the malls don't cater to hats." The store has been on Middlesex Street since its founding by his father in 1923. It is the last men's and women's hat shop in New England. Glazer attributes the shop's survival to the variety of hats. Hundreds of styles are provided to suit every taste: fedoras, homburgs, derbies, stetsons, cowboy hats, women's theatrical hats with feathers, baseball caps with sequins and rhinestones, Sherlock Holmes deerstalkers and rain hats.[15]

The forerunner of Factory Shoe Outlet on Middlesex Street owned by Barbara and Albert Bernstein was started in the early 1900s by Albert's grandfather, David, who came to Lowell from Tichin in Russia. Initially a combined shoe repair and second hand clothing store, David's children later ran the business as Bernstein Shoes. In 1932, Albert's father Harry opened his own store, Factory Shoe Outlet and it has been there ever since. Other members of the Bernstein family are still involved in retail ventures in the city.

The city's revival and redevelopment, based on the establishment of the national and state historical parks, created tourism and generated new business and service opportunities. A troubling aspect of the improvement in employment opportunities is that so many who work in Lowell choose to live in surrounding suburbs.

Hard working, ambitious, and fully accepting of the American dream, the saga of one Lowell Jewish family is with some variations the saga of many. From peddlers to merchants, carpenters to builders, middlemen waste collectors, to factory owners, newspaper distributors to publishers, and professionals, Jews were economically mobile. The case studies that follow are illustrative of this progression. Each is a prototype for others with similar stories to tell.

The present day Towers Motor Parts Corporation with branches in Lowell, Lawrence, and Nashua, New Hampshire, traces its origins to Aaron Levine, who came to Lowell in 1890 from Belarus, Russia. He was a young man with a wife and daughter whose relatives in Lowell were waiting to receive them. Aaron became an apprentice cobbler. As a sideline he began to collect discarded junk in his backyard, a large amount of which were junked cars. Aaron gave up shoemaking and began to sell automotive parts to gas stations. In 1922, his son William, with his brother-in-law, Edwin Braverman, collectively pooled their resources and bought a bankrupt filling station in which they launched an auto repair and automotive parts store—Towers Corner Auto Supply. William was the proprietor of a retail shoe store before this new venture. All of the members of the family including grandparents contributed funds to purchase the building for the present day Towers Motor Parts Corporation on Church Street in Lowell. It grew from nine employees to seventy and is today a leading supplier of automotive replacement parts in New England. William's third generation sons, Allan and Morey, both graduates of elite colleges, manage the business today. Allan and Morey's sons, however, no longer have ties to Lowell. They instead chose other professions and practice law and medicine in the Boston area.[16]

William, who died in 1990, was active in a wide range of Jewish organizations. He served as a lifetime trustee of Lowell Hebrew Community Center and Temple Beth El, as well as director of the Temple's Cemetery Corporation. He was the first president of the Lowell United Jewish Appeal and a leader of the Pouzzner B'nai B'rith lodge. He was one of the first Lowell Jews to bridge the gap and make a transition to participation in the secular institutions of the larger community as well. He was a member of the executive committee of the Lowell General Hospital, president of the Lowell Lion's Club and president of the Lowell Community Chest Association. He was a director of the Union National Bank of Lowell and, during World War II, a member of the Lowell Board of Selective Service. His social activities included serving on the executive committee of the fashionable Yorick Club and as an honorary member of the Vesper Country Club. His sons have continued on this path.

Allan has maintained many of his father's interests. He is the current President of the Merrimack Cemetery Corporation in Chelmsford, which was originally the independent order of Sons of Abraham, a cooperative burial association which was transferred to Temple Beth El in 1945. He is a recent secretary of the Lowell Harvard Club, Chairman of the Board of Trustees of the Lowell Five Cent Savings Bank, and Chairman of the United Fund. Allan was the first president of the National Automotive Trade Association.[17] The Levine family is an example of a tradition followed by many of the prosperous Jews in Lowell who, although strong supporters of Jewish organizations, also felt an obligation to contribute time and money to secular causes. The first openings for Jews in service clubs were the Lion's Club, Elks, Rotary and the Masonic Orders.

Another dramatic example of a start from humble origins is the Max Cohen family, in whose home on Howard Street in the 1890s, the Jewish community held its first minyan (religious service) which requires a minimum of ten men. Esther Cohen, Max's daughter, who died at the age of 96, recalled that her father and brothers started in business by loading a horse-drawn wagon with bottles, pots, and pans which they exchanged with families in the area for rags and scrap metal. They also bought textile waste from the mills which they resold to the paper industry.[18] The *Lowell Business Directory of 1892* lists the Cohens as "Peddlers or Junk Dealers." The *Directory of 1908* contains an advertisement for "M. Cohen and Son with Telephone Connection." The 1912 Directory lists the Cohens under the specialized heading of "bottles." From operating out of a horse-drawn cart this family business, within a ten year period, progressed to first renting and then owning a store. The entire family supported the enterprise. Esther served as the bookkeeper.

Benjamin Sandler, a retired Lowell lawyer who died in 1991, recollected that his father came alone from Lithuania to escape service in the Japanese-Russian War. In 1908, he sent for his wife and daughter who had been left behind. He first stayed with a sister in Chelsea, Massachusetts, but soon moved to Lowell, having been told shoemakers were needed there. Only five feet tall, he had been trained as a cobbler by the Russian army because he was considered too small for other jobs. His first job in Lowell was with his wife's uncle, who had a shoe repair business near the old train depot. After a few years he opened his own shoe repair store. Benjamin, his son, was born in 1909 on Howard Street in Lowell.

Benjamin and his sisters went to the nearby Lincoln Grammar School and to Lowell High School. All were professionally trained. Benjamin received a law degree in 1932 from Boston University. Soon after, he started a law practice in Lowell with a young Greek man. To launch this endeavor they pooled their combined resources of forty dollars.

As a young man, Benjamin lived in one of two three-decker-houses that his father owned in the heart of the old Jewish section near the orthodox Montefiore Synagogue. Upon his marriage in 1940, Benjamin moved to the more fashionable middle class Highlands area and became a member of the conservative Temple Beth El. Active in many Jewish organizations, Sandler became president of the Benjamin Pouzzner B'nai B'rith lodge in 1939. By contrast, his father only had time to make a living. He ventured into real estate, owning his own house and renting another for additional income, and fulfilled the dream of having his children properly educated.[19] Resources accumulated from real estate investments were often used to further the education of one's children.

Some who succeeded were entirely self-made. While still an adolescent, Nathan Cohen had to go to work to help support his family. His father came to Lowell in 1897 to escape call-up as a reservist with the Czarist army. He barely made a living by engaging in the marginal activity of buying and selling used goods. Watching his father struggle, Nathan was determined to prosper. He started a small paper business in Lowell in 1920 which was incorporated as the Merrimack Paper Tube Company in 1929. Nathan owned this thriving business until his retirement in 1974.[20]

The most successful dealer in industrial waste was David Ziskind, whose profits from a successful junk business were reinvested in the purchase of declining properties. A model venture capitalist, he and his son Jacob bought old mills in Lowell and in other parts of the country. As entrepreneurs, they continually bought used textile equipment. Some of the reclaimed machinery was resold to companies in Latin

America. The Ziskinds became multi-millionaires. The fortune acquired enabled the Ziskind family to become the leading philanthropists in Lowell. Jacob is credited with taking many businesses on the brink of disaster and revitalizing them. The pattern of mill purchases he established consisted of surveying a mill which was for sale, evaluating the machinery and assessing whether there should be a resale of the plant equipment or a rehabilitation of the entire mill. He built an industrial empire based on his keen understanding of the market, both domestic and foreign. An example of Jacob's success in Lowell was his takeover of the Merrimack Manufacturing Company in the 1940s when it was in physical and operational decline. He replenished the machinery, increased its work force from 1,000 to 2,200 and increased profits in one year from six million to fourteen million dollars. On occasion Ziskind's entrepreneurship went far afield—even extending to the purchase of the Edwards Company in Cleveland, Ohio, one of the countries oldest wholesale grocers.[21]

At the time of Jacob's untimely death in 1950 at the age of fifty-one, he was the President of the Merrimack Manufacturing Company. The employees, desiring to honor his memory, established a memorial scholarship in his name at Lowell Technological Institute to enable a student from Lowell or its surrounding towns to attend the school. The Jacob Ziskind Foundation has over the years distributed millions of dollars to educational and medical institutions.

The Solomont brothers, Joseph, Meyer and Sy, were born in Boston's North End. Their father, Todras, who had earlier emigrated from Russia, came to Lowell with his wife, Elkeh, and their three sons to open a fish market. At age 18, Todras, along with thirty other young men, was arrested in Valkenek, Russia, by Czarist secret police for having in their possession literature that was considered revolutionary and, therefore, forbidden. For this offense, he was sent to a prison in Siberia. As a political prisoner, he was later pardoned and chose to leave the country for America.[22] All of his sons were industrious and hardworking. Joseph, the oldest, graduated from Lowell High school and started at Northeastern University, from which he dropped out and went to work in a sweater factory in Lowell to help support his parents. Meyer, without any undergraduate schooling, went to law school and passed the bar exam. The three brothers were always in business together, sharing their profits and losses.

Over the years the brothers engaged in a variety of enterprises. Among them were real estate ventures, an Army and Navy store, drive-in movies and a night club. They also served as entertainment impresarios and secondary financiers. They hit their stride in the 1940s with the takeover and operation of nursing homes throughout the Merrimack Valley. Willow Manor, the kosher nursing home they established in Lowell, serves even today as a community center. Joseph's son, Alan, mused that his father and his uncles always felt insecure and perceived themselves as poor kids. He recounted that his father was surprised to receive a bank loan from Homer Bourgeois, president of Union National Bank (now Fleet Bank). Joseph knew that prominent men had been turned down. While he nervously waited to see Bourgeois, an important old Yankee came out of the president's office and stated that Homer was "one hard man." Joseph got his loan as well as praise from Bourgeois with regard to his business ethics.[23]

The third generation children are all college educated. Joseph's four sons have successfully pioneered and put into practice new concepts in state-of-the-art health care and assisted-living units for the elderly. Meyer's son, David, is the current president of Montefiore synagogue. Mindful of their own journey from poverty to privilege, Joseph, Meyer and Sy established a charitable trust in memory of their immigrant parents. It provides funds worldwide to support Jewish education. This foundation is largely responsible for rebuilding the orthodox Montefiore Synagogue and for establishing the Merrimack Valley Jewish Academy in Lowell. The fund has also endowed nursing scholarships at the University of Massachusetts Lowell. All three brothers have held leadership positions in the establishment and the continuing programs of the Montefiore Synagogue. Meyer was the first president of the new synagogue and Sy was chairman of the building committee.

Allan believes the Solomont family maintained its strong ties to Jewish orthodoxy as a conscious way of perpetuating their sense of belonging. Strict adherence to Torah decrees ensured group survival. Strong patriarchal ties and the following of traditions remained in place from grandfathers to fathers and sons.[24]

Frank Goldman was a most distinguished member of the Jewish community who practiced law in Lowell for fifty years. He gained worldwide recognition as a Jewish leader from 1947 until 1953 when he served as the International President of B'nai B'rith. His son, Robert, who died in 1991, also maintained a law office in Lowell. Robert was the valedictorian of his class at Lowell High School, a graduate of Harvard University Law School and a law clerk for the distinguished Judge Learned Hand. Both father and son were legal counselors to the *Lowell Sun* newspaper. The Goldman family started from humble beginnings. Frank's father had come to Lowell from Poland/Lithuania in 1880 to open a clothing store.[25]

An inspiring example of the continuing immigrant saga was dramatized in June, 1994. An exhibit opened at the Mogan Cultural Center in Lowell, "Browsing Through Birke's," which focused on the history of Nathan and Sally Birke and the department store they opened on Central Street in Lowell in 1948. The Birkes were Holocaust survivors from Poland who fled to the U.S. in 1945 to begin a new life. With nearly their entire families murdered in the Nazi death camps, they arrived penniless and established one of the most popular discount clothing stores in Lowell. The store had the look of an old country store in the city with the difference—it sold designer-type clothes at bargain prices.[26]

In Poland, Nathan had been a wealthy businessman, yet his first job in Lowell was as a janitor at Temple Beth El. Nathan died in 1992 at age eighty-four; his wife Sally continues to manage the store now located on Market Street in the heart of the city. Nathan, a colorful character, held court seated at a metal table in the center of the store where coffee and cookies were provided to all who wanted to join with him in meaningful conversation about world events. Birke vowed to never forget the Holocaust; newspaper articles and Holocaust photographs were stapled to the walls of the store. A gruff man, Nathan didn't suffer fools easily or have patience for those customers who simply wanted to browse. Everyone shopped at

Birke's from up-scale professionals to former mill workers. All report that Birke's clothes wore like iron and could be passed down to younger family members.[27]

Nathan's daughter Szifra, who is a health therapist and the guiding force behind the exhibit, reminisces that Nathan spent nothing on himself but was passionate about providing funds for his four children to go to college.[28]

Not all Jews achieved dramatic success but most did well enough collecting waste and recycling, operating small stores and serving as middlemen wholesalers to provide a springboard for their children to acquire better lives. Parents were strong and ardent supporters of the public schools and sent their children to them as a way of insuring they would adapt to American cultural patterns and mix with other American youth. Children were encouraged to do well and, upon graduating from Lowell High School, a good number attended Ivy League colleges.

As Jews prospered, they were expected to contribute to the Jewish community. They were thus actively involved in Jewish fraternal organizations as well as strong supporters of the local synagogues—many belonging to more than one.

Those who started as peddlers had little overhead and thus were able to save to open small grocery and dry-good stores. Some who became merchants were lent money by family members or the local free loan societies. Still others first worked as clerks or bookkeepers in businesses of their relatives and later ventured out on their own. Close proximity to each other facilitated exchange of information and access to business opportunities. Jews recognized the value of owning property. Capital from real estate investments was often a crucial means of increasing one's wealth. By 1910, most of the buildings in the Jewish section were Jewish owned and some Jews were building contractors. Often a family would buy a tenement building, live on one floor and rent rooms on the other floors.

Overall, Lowell Jews were adventurous. Many left inner city ghettoes such as the North End of Boston to seek opportunities where, faced with less competition, they could explore new territory for peddling. They left the security of living in large, closely knit Jewish settlements to go where they would have increased chances of becoming proprietors and professionals. They believed the small city would provide sufficient room to absorb all those who wanted to come. The small size of the Jewish community facilitated acceptance by non-Jews. Jews lived in close proximity to other groups. Each of the ethnic settlements bordered on the others. From the earliest time there was some interaction among Jews and other immigrants. Jews in their roles as shopkeepers interacted with those in other groups and thus helped erode unfavorable stereotypes. Yet Jews felt they were viewed with some ambivalence and perceived as outsiders. Perhaps it related to the fact that Jews did not remain long as wage laborers engaged in the main occupation of mill work, as did those in other groups. Jews overwhelmingly embraced the American ideal that hard work and discipline would bring rewards. Jews had a strong propensity towards commerce and self employment. They are a visible example of a collective move up the economic class ladder because, for many, occupational goals of self employment for themselves and professional status for their children rapidly was achieved. Earlier generations provided a cushion for furthering the well being of later generations. By and large, Jews perceived themselves as businessmen, not workers. They prided themselves on taking care of their own. No Jew was on the city welfare rolls. They provided social services and helped each other with informal sources of credit.

Self employment for Jews had been a rational response to various forms of discrimination in the labor market. The old, self-employed, small businesmen needed hard work, savings and fortitude. The later professional generations had to rely on educational achievement and recognized credentials.

Notes

1. Nathan Glazer and Daniel P. Moynihan, *Beyond the Melting Pot*, 2nd Edition Cambridge: M.I.T. Press, 1970 p. 143.
2. Glazer and Moynihan.
3. Alejandro Porter and Leif Jensen, "What's an Ethnic Enclave? The Case for Conceptual Clarity," *American Sociological Review*, Vol. 52, Number 6, December 1987, p. 68.
4. *Lowell Sun*, "Clothing Store Looking for a new Home," December 30, 1985 , and Interview with Herman Lemkin, Shirley Kolack, July, 1995.
5. Herman Lemkin, 1995.
6. Interview with Mirian Chosoid, Shirley Kolack, 1989.
7. Nancy Tuttle, "Picture It: Lowell Goes to the Movies," *Exhibit Booklet*, Patrick Mogan Cultural Center, 1993.
8. Mario Shav, "Emerging Business," *Boston Globe*, December 8, 1993.
9. Marc Scott Miller, *The Irony of Victory: World War I and Lowell, Massachusetts* University of Illinois Press, 1988 p. 115.
10. Among the first lawyers, all of whom remained in Lowell were: Bennett Silverblatt, Morris Balofsky, Benjamin Sandler and Frank Goldman.
11. Oral History Interview, Mary Blewett (for Lowell National Historical Park), 1985.
12. Interview with Benjamin Sandler, Shirley Kolack, 1989.
13. Interview with Fanny Moore, Shirley Kolack, June, 1994.
14. Interview with Len Gravitz, Former Executive Director, Merrimack Valley Combined Jewish Philanthrophies, Shirley Kolack, 1989.
15. *Boston Sunday Globe*, "Pick of the Weekly Tops in Hats," November 8, 1992, and interview with Melvin Glazer, Shirley Kolack, 1995.
16. Interview with Allan Levine, Shirley Kolack, August, 1994.
17. Allan Levine, 1994.
18. Interview with Esther Cohen, Mark Levine, 1987.
19. Benjamin Sandler, 1989.

20. Interview with Nathan Cohen, Center for Lowell History; University of Massachusetts Lowell, 1985.
21. *American Wool and Cotton Reporter*, A Tribute to Jacob Ziskind, October 26, 1950.
22. Anna May Zimman, *I Remember,* (Boston: H.O. Zimman, Inc., 1988) pp. 28-30.
23. Interview with Alan Solomont, August, 1994.
24. Alan Solomont, 1994.
25. Interview with Robert Goldman, Shirley Kolack, 1988.
26. "Browsing Through Birke's," An Exhibit by Szifra Birke, Patrick J. Mogan Cultural Center, Lowell, June 25-August 30, 1994.
27. "Browsing Through Birke's."
28. Interview with Szifra Birke, Shirley Kolack, 1995.

Chapter 5

ADAPTATION

Jews represented a cohesive, self-contained group long after they became a merchant class of store owners, professionals, managers and technicians. Physically isolated from the larger Jewish community of greater Boston, Lowell Jews did not venture out of the city for their social activities. Only in later years did the Jewish community become more fragmented, with the widespread use of cars providing easy mobility.

Judith Green Chaloff, who was a teenager in the 1950s, recalled that social activities at Temple Beth El and the Jewish Community Center were the focal point of social life for Jewish young people. The girls, ages 15-18, belonged to the Hadassah youth organization, the Hadassah Buds; the boys, ages 16-21, to Aleph Zadek Aleph (AZA), the youth component of B'nai B'rith. She states that there were about sixty Jewish students at Lowell High, all in the college preparatory tract. There were voluntary group-imposed ethnic cliques and each group socialized separately.[1]

Jewish culture remained alive throughout the years, supported by the Jewish theater, the sisterhood and brotherhood programs of the synagogues, and the fundraising activities of the various organizations for local and worldwide Jewish causes. Help with funding of Jewish projects in Palestine was especially popular. A 1916 play bill for the popular play *Shoshana* was written in English, Hebrew and Yiddish. Performed in Lowell, the play extolled the values of American pluralism within the framework of maintaining group belonging. Its themes were an endorsement of capitalism, self-help and the goal of upward social mobility. During the devastating years of the great depression (1930s), the play *Don't Foreclose on Us*, a production of the drama group of the Jewish Community Center, was performed. It reflected the dire situation at the time of many local Jewish businesses.

During this period of economic crisis, members of the synagogues found themselves financially strapped. Temple Beth El had to cut the salary of Rabbi Joseph Warren who had come to the congregation in December, 1929. The services of a cantor were discontinued. The treasurer of the synagogue paid the religious school teachers with loans from his own pocket and members of the congregation were allowed to pay their annual dues in small weekly installments. The Jewish community's devotion to maintaining its institutions is illustrated by Temple Beth El meeting its operating obligations. The religious school functioned, religious services were held and Bar Mitzvah boys confirmed.

Throughout the years, Rose Goldman, wife of Frank Goldman, composed poems for important Jewish ceremonial events. Her poem *America*, which is printed in the Lowell Hebrew Community Center commemorative booklet of 1927, highlights the belief in a bright future for all in this blessed land.

America

God planned a realm of Beauty,
Girded by mountain and sea,
He drew it majestic in Beauty,
Sturdy and wondrous to see.

God loved the plan in His Vision,
Perfected His work from above,
Blessed every place of His Vision,
Glorified it with His love.

God set this land to the Westward,
In that Morning of Mystery,
Blessed the Great Land to the Westward,
Gave it to men who are Free.

Pearl Styman reminisced about a social group that, until 1992, met once a month to keep Yiddish language and culture alive. Some of its members have died or moved to Florida and now the group only meets sporadically, valiantly continuing its mission. Her father, Hyman Shapman, born in Russsia, came to Lowell in 1918 to open a kosher butcher shop. His shop became a social center. It served as an informal collection station for various charities including money for various rabbis who came to town seeking help for congregations in other places. At one time there were three such butcher shops, the last of which closed in the mid-1960s. Pearl believes this was a result of the decline of tightly-knit Jewish neighborhoods and more assimilated children moving to the suburbs.[2]

In the past, Lowell exemplified the inevitability of the strong sense of community that prevails in a small city or town where one knows every fellow Jew and has more than likely participated in all the major life passages and ceremonial occasions. It was expected that when someone was sick, died or gave birth, the entire community would participate in the sadness or joy.

Allan Levine stated that Jews in Boston thought of Jews in Lowell as living in the hinterlands—a world apart.[3] Jews in Lowell, sensing their isolation, felt in turn a strong need to keep their Jewish identity alive. Over time they sought to maintain a delicate balance between adaptation and distinctiveness. Adherence to traditional Jewish religious practices was a given in the early generations but has been replaced today by greater tolerance for individual choices. There are fewer Jews today who strictly observe dietary laws, which undoubtedly is one of the causes for the demise of kosher butcher stores and bakeries. A reaffirmation of Jewish communal ties has occurred due to the trauma for Jews of the Nazi Holocaust and the overwhelming support for the establishment of the state of Israel.

A focus of group cohesiveness and turning inward occurs whenever a people feel threatened by attacks from the outside. Jews in Lowell always had a sense of marginality reinforced by national anti-Semitism. There was never organized anti-Jewish sentiment in the city but Jewish men who grew up in the pre World War II years remembered that as young boys on their way to school, they were taunted by Irish and French boys with the epitaph "Christ killers."[4] There were no Jewish teachers to serve as role models in the schools. With the economic improvement of Jewish families and their adaptation to the city, this open hostility ceased. The old Protestant and Irish residents however did continue to resent the invasion of new immigrants into their neighborhoods but Lowell was composed of so many different ethnic enclaves it became difficult to single out any one group for discrimination. All, however reluctant, were required in this mill-dominated city to live a multi-cultural existence. There was a juxtaposition of many cultural groups, and the residents of each group remained largely self segregated. There was always a flood of anti-immigrant feeling that greeted the arrival of each new immigrant group. The fear of the newcomers revolved partly around the struggle over jobs. There was a constant influx of new groups, always desperate for work.[5]

Frederick Coburn in *History of Lowell and Its People* states that around 1890 many of the thousands of Russian and Polish Jews who were coming into New York were finding their way into the Merrimack Valley. There was fear in Lowell that, as a result, hundreds of people already settled in the area would be out of employment. Solidarity of the workers and formation of unions were held back by the fact that native born Americans and the Irish hesitated to fraternize with French-Canadians, Greeks, and Hebrews. There was always a concern that the newcomers would provide a cheaper supply of labor.[6]

By the turn of the century, the Irish in Lowell began to rise in status and influence due partly to their large numbers. The Irish had been greeted initially with fear and suspicion on the part of the Yankee Protestants. The French in turn felt they were victims of Irish prejudice and accused the Irish of deliberately mispronouncing their French names. They also expressed dislike of the Irish domination of the Catholic Church. Just as the arrival of the French-Canadians strengthened the position of the Irish, the arrival of the southeastern and eastern Europeans increased the security of the French-Canadians, who viewed the new immigrants as belonging to a less desirable class. The French in the mill towns of the Merrimack region singled out the Jews for particularly vicious attacks. The basis of the conflict appeared to be economic.[7]

During the great depression years leading up to World War II, there was growing anti-Semitic activity in Boston from which there were spinoffs into peripheral towns. It was a period of isolationism in American society. Nationally, Father Charles Coughlin, a mentor of the Christian Front, used the radio to spew forth his hatred of Jews with canards of an international Jewish conspiracy. In addition, between 1940 and 1942, Coughlin's weekly newspaper *Social Justice*, with a circulation of over one million, carried stories accusing Jews of starting World War II.[8] Benjamin Sandler recalled with pride that he and other members of the Pouzzner B'nai B'rith Lodge of Lowell volunteered to go as observers to local churches on Sundays to listen and respond to anti-Semitic speakers who were sent by followers of Coughlin to spread his outrageous views that Jews were dragging the United States into war.[9] Coughlin's diatribes came to an end in 1942 when he was forced by his superior, Cardinal Edward Mooney, to cease his nonreligious activities or face suspension from the priesthood. The vicious attacks on Jews by the Coughlinites and the Christian Front had led to assaults on Jewish youths throughout the country. The Boston diocesan newspaper, the *Pilot*, was especially strong in its opposition to Jews and its support for Father Coughlin.[10]

As an antidote to anti-Semitism and the need for resettlement of the remnants of displaced European Jews following World War II, Lowell Jews became ardent supporters of the Zionist Organization of America (ZOA). Its focus was on Israel and its survival. Sidney Rindler, a Jewish lawyer who was a leader of the Lowell Zionist movement, recalled that in the 1940s Temple Beth El had written into its by-laws the stipulation that dues for the ZOA be incorporated into the temple's membership fees. Thus a large amount of money was raised for the ZOA.[11]

A crucial legacy of World War II was the erosion of group boundaries in Lowell. Contacts beyond work settings were strengthened. Some Jews became members of prestigious Christian social clubs. The Pouzzner B'nai B'rith Lodge gave its coveted brotherhood award to Cardinal Richard Cushing in 1957.

Cushing was appointed archbishop of Boston in 1944. He vigorously condemned anti-Semitism, and today Catholics and Jews in Massachusetts have good relations. An important theme of the war was that Americans were fighting for survival, and a common American identity that transcended each group's special self interests was fostered. The German and Japanese war machines were viewed as a threat to the existence of all. One hundred and fifty young Jewish men from Lowell served in the armed forces. Prior to World War II, Jewish involvement with non-Jews had been minimal and formal. Jews now joined in the activities of a wide range of community organizations.

In part due to their small community size, Jews never ran for political office nor did they wish to be viewed as a separate ethnic or religious bloc. They first openly participated in politics when they actively got out the vote for Franklin Delano Roosevelt, commencing with his first campaign for the presidency in 1932. Roosevelt was viewed as having concern for the plight of European Jewry.

Jews gradually adapted their religious practices to accommodate their new environment. Having acquired greater acceptance and no longer poor and powerless, they were faced, for the first time, with how to maintain their identity as a matter of choice rather than birth. A particular observance of rituals and a traditional Jewish way of life was followed based on one's initially-ascribed status. In closed and pervasively anti-Semitic European societies, it would have been rare for a Jew to question his group affiliation. One was a Jew because one's parents were Jews and one was raised as a Jew. Also, hostile Christians would not let Jews shed their identity.

There had been two institutional strains of Jewishness for the immigrant Jews. There were those who only accepted a secular Jewish cultural identity represented by such groups as the Arbiter Ring (Workmen's Circle), which was committed to the betterment of workers. By contrast, most other Jews were deeply pious and religiously orthodox. In Lowell, the Workmen's Circle now is remembered only for the medical and burial benefits it provided its members. Jews were too busy eking out a living to embrace the socialist-utopian ideals of this worker's group. Even when they were working class, they perceived themselves as middle class and encouraged middle class ambitions among their children. As part of their adjustment to American society, they endorsed the philosophy of capitalism with its emphasis on competition and individual responsibility. They fervently believed that to acquire education was a precondition for gaining status and prosperity.

The changes in the nature of synagogue affiliation reflects adjustment patterns among Jews. Originally, there were a multitude of tiny shuls (synagogues) which permitted each man to worship in the style familiar to him in his European place of origin. A religious service could be conducted in any place where there was a minyan present (ten Jewish men); the leaders were not necessarily trained rabbis. Religious rituals and practices evolved into the establishment of only three synagogues, each representing one of the major strains of Judaism—orthodox, conservative and reform—and each with a seminary trained rabbi. The independent cemetery and burial society lodges were integrated into the synagogue structures. An important, unifying development was the merging of Temple Beth El Synagogue and the Jewish Community Center. This union provided an intimate connection between religious practices and community activities. Organizational life expanded from landsmenschaft groups (people from same villages in Europe or extended families) to affiliation with Jewish organizations on a national level. Prominent national figures were invited to come to Lowell to stimulate interest in Jewish causes and to offer advice to the local chapters of national organizations. In 1921, the B'nai B'rith Pouzzner Lodge held a banquet in Page's Dining Room in Lowell to honor the internationally famous Rabbi Steven Wise, one of the earliest American Zionists and a leading proponent of social reform. He was the keynote speaker for the evening.

Ties were also strengthened with Boston when Jewish leaders came to Lowell to install organizational officers. One old resident reported that Jackson Holtz, a distinguished Boston lawyer, was dazzled and impressed with the sophistication and crudition of the young women of Junior Hadassah when he came to install their officers on a date that coincided with the celebration of the holiday of Purim. The entertainment for the evening was a presentation of an adaptation of the saga of the festival of Purim with a mock trial of Haman, the chief minister of King Ahasueros of Persia, who plotted the destruction of the Persian Jews and was thwarted in his attempt by the Jewish Queen Esther.

An annual ceremony that reflects the patriotic sentiments of Jewish war veterans and serves to strengthen their ties to all veterans is held each year on Memorial Day, under the leadership of Donald Van Greenby, a World War II veteran. Services are held at the Jewish cemeteries in Pelham, New Hampshire, and Chelmsford, Massachusetts, to honor all the war dead. Donald's father, David Van Greenby, was a major in World War I and the Lowell Jewish War Veterans post is named in his honor.

For Jews in Lowell, as in the country as a whole, there has been a continuing delicate balance of assimilation and maintaining distinctiveness.[12] For the first and second generations, there would have been strict adherence to dietary laws, religious rituals and practices. Later generations have been less consistent in their observances.

Over the years the observance of some religious holidays have become more Americanized. The celebration of the holiday of Chanukah illustrates one such adaptation. The Feast of Lights, or Chanukah, was traditionally a minor holiday commemorating the victory of the Maccabees over the Hellenized Syrians in 165 B.C.E. and the rededication of the temple in Jerusalem to the worship of God. The eight day festival is symbolized by lighting one candle each night in a menorah (a candelabra) and on the final night all eight candles glow. As part of the home ceremony, special Chanukah songs are sung, children receive nightly gifts and there are special food delights, such as potato latkes (pancakes). Chanukah occurs at approximately the same time as Christmas and both solstice holidays share ornamental lights and gift giving. Thus the kindling of the Chanukah lights becomes a way of providing a winter festival for Jewish children to coincide with Christmas. American Jews can also identify the Macabees who saved the ancient temple with the soldiers of modern Israel.

Passover, which occurs in the spring season, as does Easter, remains one of the more enduring and beloved holidays.

Both Easter and Passover in popular culture celebrate a renewal. Passover recalls the story through the Seder, a participatory service around the dinner table, that recounts the great exodus of Jews from Egypt in 1200 B.C.E. and how Jews were freed from slavery. Passover has universal themes of freedom that are applicable to American values and the experiences of other ethnic and minority groups. Often non-Jewish friends are invited to participate in the Seder meal. Traditional foods are still served, such as soup with knadlach (dumplings) and Matzoh (unleavened bread). An adaptation for some Jews is having the Seder only on the first night of Passover instead of two nights. The holiday lasts for eight days.

There is a renewed interest in the holiday of Succoth, originally a celebration of the harvest and a commemoration of the 40 years' wandering of the Jews in Biblical times. The building of a succah an outdoor shelter with a natural roof of leafy branches through which the sky can be seen is an enjoyable family ritual. Succahs are often decorated with children's art, hanging fruits and corn stalks—symbols associated with the American holiday of Thanksgiving. During the seven day holiday, families eat their meals and some even sleep in the succah. Today, there are thriving businesses that sell prefabricated succcah kits. Bert Paley recalls that his father Morris Palefsky who was one of the early builders in Lowell, supplied the synagogues with the heavy wooden panels that early traditional Jews used for the three sides of the succahs.

The most solemn and holy days remain the high holidays Rosh Hashonah commemorates the Jewish New Year, ending ten days later with Yom Kippur, the day of Atonement. This is a day of fasting and praying when one asks for forgiveness from God for offenses against one's fellow man. These days are the holidays that are most observed and sanctified. As in the past synagogues remain filled to overflowing. Traditional Jews observe Rosh Hashonah for two days. Reform Jews observe a single day.

The traditional observations of the Sabbath, Friday night at sundown and Saturday, have changed for many. Fewer attend Friday night synagogue services that usher in the Sabbath. Nor is the Sabbath observed as a day of prayer and rest for all as it would have been for the early Jewish arrivals. The reason that Jews abandoned work in the mills was often the discomfort pious Jews experienced when forced to work on Saturdays and thus violate their Sabbath. An industrialized society, with its emphasis on the profit motive and competition, placed a heavy burden on those who tried to live by upholding religious practices and obligations that were in conflict with the processes of modernization.

The European Jews who came to Lowell were largely orthodox and it would have been socially unacceptable not to abide by dietary laws and to strictly observe the Sabbath. According to Jewish law, all Jews are supposed to observe kashrut. This entails eating only kosher meat (meat that has been slaughtered according to religious ritual). Meat and milk products are not to be prepared or eaten together (Thou shall not boil a kid in its mother's milk, Exodus 23:19). Also prescribed is to have two sets of dishes and cooking utensils—one for meat and the other for dairy. Only fish with fins and scales may be eaten. When not available locally, kosher food would be brought in from Boston.

In Europe, Jews had lived in enclosed enclaves surrounded by other Jews and this is the environment they recreated in America. However, American secular values took their toll and there was a decline in the elaborate preparation for the Sabbath. Now coming back in vogue however, is the lovely ritual of lighting the Sabbath candles and reciting the Hebrew blessings at the start of the special Friday night dinner. The Jewish holidays that are celebrated in the home are proving to be the most enduring.

Still today during the four Sundays of the Jewish month of Elul—which falls in September or October, Jews go to cemeteries to pay homage and remember the deceased. Most place small pebbles from the ground on top of the graves to signify they were visited. Mendel Banks, who became financial secretary of the Israel Brotherhood in 1957 (the original cemetery society for the Pelham, New Hampshire, cemetery), recalled that even Jews who have moved far away from Lowell returned to the cemetery during this period to renew their roots. He recounted that one woman comes each year from Brooklyn, New York, to visit her father's grave. Even though it is a hardship, she comes and returns the same day. There are traditional symbols on many of the headstones, such as candelabra for women, symbolizing their role in lighting sabbath candles, and hands for men who were the descendents of the Kohens, the ancient high priests of the Hebrews. Grave epitaphs are in Yiddish and Hebrew.[13]

Each of the ethnic groups began their sojourn in Lowell within the closed boundaries of church and neighborhood. Groups were mentally and physically separated. How isolated each group remained for a long period of time is expressed by a Greek woman who reported:

> The Polish would stay in Centralville, the French at Moody Street, so everybody had their own group, their own area. The Greeks kept together, just like the Frenchmen kept together, or the Portuguese, or the Irish or whatever. We stuck together. We didn't go outside our area. I was quite old when I first went downtown.[14]

Some Jews, however, did venture forth. Sidney Rindler recalled that his father, an immigrant from Austria, came to Lowell in 1913 to join other relatives. The Rindler family settled in the Polish area where they opened a general store. The Rindlers spoke Polish and therefore found this provided a great advantage for serving the Poles. Sidney, who is now eighty-five, reminisced that his family maintained cordial relations with their neighbors and customers, and their business flourished. Deeply devout, the entire family, with his mother pushing a baby carriage, would walk the long distance to the synagogue in the Jewish section on the Sabbath and the high holidays.[15] Meaningful intergroup contacts first began with business associations.

Rabbi Chaim Goldberger of the orthodox Montefiore Synagogue believes that an ecumenical spirit now prevails in Lowell and that there is mutual respect among Jews and the other ethnic groups. The mayor of Lowell, Richard Howe, was present at Rabbi Goldberger's installation and presented the rabbi with a plaque of welcome from the city.[16] In an earlier era, no official notice would have been made of the arrival of a new rabbi. Rabbi Goldberger points out that among his congregants there are younger Jews who desire by choice to return to traditional rituals and practices as a way of maintaining Jewish continuity. The demands of industrialization loosened some ties and left later generations with a spiritual emptiness they now seek to redress.

Perhaps the most poignant recent acceptance of change and adaptation is the appointment of a young woman rabbi at Temple Beth El. Rabbi Leslie Gordon was appointed to this position in June of 1994. A member of long standing conceded that he initially dreaded the Temple search committee's selection of Rabbi Gordon. He feared he would be unable to adjust to this break with tradition. He quickly added however that in a brief period, the rabbi has performed well and is the Temple's best asset. Rabbi Gordon has generated excitement and renewed vitality among Temple members.

Overall Lowell Jews have accommodated well to conditions they faced in the new land. They sought to perpetuate their religious values and practices while also embracing many aspects of the dominant culture of the American way of life. Paradoxically, Jews in small cities such as Lowell tenaciously tried to maintain Jewish identity more so than in large urban areas. They extended themselves to all Jewish institutions as a way of defining themselves. The important bond of organizations, some philanthropic, others educational, some supporting Israel, others supporting causes closer to home, united the community. Karen Hockberg, the wife of a former Montefiore Rabbi, summed up this unity when she mused, "one thing that Lowell doesn't lack is organizations. Lowell is really organization-minded."[17]

Notes

1. Interview with Judith Green Chaloff, Shirley Kolack, 1989.
2. Interview with Pearl Styman, Shirley Kolack, 1988.
3. Interview with Allan Levine, Shirley Kolack, 1994.
4. Group Interview with Senior Citizens, Willow Manor Nursing and Retirement Center, Lowell, MA, Shirley Kolack, 1988.
5. Shirley Kolack, "Lowell an Immigrant City, The Old and the New" in *Sourcebook on the New Immigration*, Roy Bryce Laporte, ed. (New Brunswick, New Jersey: Transaction Books, 1980) p. 340.
6. Frederick W. Coburn, *History of Lowell and its People* (New York: Lowell Historical Publications, 1920) pp. 344-345.
7. *Le Progres*, February 7, 1902, May 14, 1903, April 5, 1906 (cited in Donald Cole), *Immigrant City* (Chapel Hill: University of North Carolina Press) 1963.
8. Lenard Dinnerstein, *Anti-semitism in America* (New York: Oxford University Press, 1994) p. 132.
9. Interview with Benjamin Sandler, Shirley Kolack, 1989.
10. Dinnerstein, pp. 132-133.
11. Interview with Sidney Rindler, December, 1994.
12. Note: The following discussion of adaptation of Jews in relation to religious rituals and practices is substantiated in: Albert Gordon, *Jews in Transition* (Minneapolis: University of Minnesota Press, 1949) Marshall Sklare and Joseph Greenblum, *The Lakeville Studies* (New York: Basic Books, 1967) Robert Brym, William Shaffer and Morton Weinfeld, eds., *The Jews in Canada* (Toronto: Oxford University Press, 1993)
13. Interview with Mendel Banks, Martha Norkunas, 1987, Lowell Folklife Project, American Folklife Center; Library of Congress.
14. Martha Norkunas, "The Ethnic Enclave as Cultural Space: Women's Oral Histories of Life and Work in Lowell," in *The Continuing Revolution*, Robert Weible, ed., Lowell Historical Society, 1991, p. 332.
15. Interview with Sidney Rindler, Shirley Kolack, December, 1994.
16. Interview with Rabbi Chaim Goldberger, Shirley Kolack, August, 1994.
17. *Lowell Sun*, "Jews had a role in Lowell's History," September 30, 1976.

Notes

Chapter 6

PRESENT STATUS AND THE FUTURE

There will always be a Jewish presence in Lowell. In 1907 and 1908, the *American Jewish Year Book* estimated the Jewish population at 1,200. Some years later the Jewish population reached its peak when the *American Jewish Year Book* of 1919 and 1920 listed Lowell with a Jewish population of 6,000 and a variety of organizations.[1] After 1920, the Jewish population stabilized at approximately 2,000. There has undoubtedly been a slow decline since World War II. This in part relates to the general lack of opportunity in old New England mill towns and the departure of Jews in general from small towns. It is also a story of fathers who built businesses for sons who did not want them and, after acquiring an education, opted for careers in the professions instead.

Lowell experienced a golden age from the 1820s through the 1840s when the cotton mills were booming and faced no competition. Periods of prosperity and depression followed this era. The fortunes of Jews, as that of other ethnic groups, ebbed and flowed with the economic well being of the city. During the World War II years, Jews rented floors of abandoned mills to engage in manufacturing materials that were needed for the war. The years following the war were often bleak.

In the 1970s, a revival began with the establishment of a computer industry in the city. Wang Laboratories located its international headquarters in Lowell. Growth in the high technology industry continued and in the 1980s spread to the areas surrounding Lowell. This, combined with federal and state funded historic preservation projects in the city, led to a revitalization which reversed a long period of decline. However, in the 1990s, economic problems have once again arisen.[2] In 1994, Wang sold its corporate headquarters, having downsized its activities to developing computer software only. The new owners of the property, Cross Point, have already leased two of the buildings to NYNEX with plans for several additional corporations to occupy the third and fourth buildings. The entire complex will be a state-of-the-art multiple-use center with a gift shop, travel agency, day care center and restaurants occupying ground level floors. Once again, there is hope for a revitalization of this historic city—a repeat of the cycle of resuscitation after decline.

The revival of the city in the 1970s brought in a sizable number of young Jewish families whose breadwinners were engineers and computer experts as well as members of the faculty and staff of the expanding University of Massachusetts Lowell campus. There were also Jewish physicians affiliated with the local hospitals. Just as the earlier Jews, some of these newcomers have settled in the Highlands area near the Beth El and Montefiore Synagogues. Their presence provides an element of sorely needed Jewish continuity for the membership of the synagogues. Though the membership in both synagogues is stable at this time, a large number of the members are over sixty.[3] Many of the older generation have retired and moved away or died. Some have moved to the surrounding suburbs and joined synagogues in these communities.

However, even those who leave Lowell for the contiguous suburbs still maintain work and family ties to those in Lowell. There remains a strong sense of community. Many Jewish families in Lowell intramarried due to their daily synagogue, organizational, business and social contacts. This in turn molded them into a cohesive group with extended family overtones. Close kinship connections have made for a united fellowship. There is a high rate of synagogue affiliation and, despite philosophical and doctrinal differences, quite a few are dual members of Montefiore and Temple Beth El Synagogues. There is also a core of children and grandchildren of the immigrant generation who had opportunity to pursue careers elsewhere but chose to stay in Lowell because of their attachment to the city and the close bonds to synagogues and friends.

Bernard Shapiro, a math professor at the University of Massachusetts Lowell, graduated from Lowell High School in 1950. As a youth, he worked after school in his father's grocery store. His father, Morris, was born in Vilna, Lithuania, in 1884, and was naturalized in Lowell in 1924. The grocery store expanded into a small supermarket. Bernard's father died in 1950 and it was assumed that after acquiring a college education Bernard would return to join his mother and brother in the family run store. Bernard became one of the proprietors of the business in 1958 but was unhappy and left in 1964 to begin his teaching career at the university. In the intervening years he had been a Naval Academy cadet, attended Lowell Textile Institute and received a graduate degree from Massachusetts Institute of Technology. Bernard never regretted his decision to become a professor and to continue to live in Lowell. He and his wife, Diana, who was born in Haverhill, a nearby industrial city in many ways similar to Lowell, found Lowell a good place to raise their three children. All three are Lowell High graduates and college graduates—one daughter is now a major in the U.S. Air Force. She has an undergraduate degree from the University of Massachusetts Lowell; the other daughter has an engineering degree from the University of Massachusetts Amherst. Bernard looks back fondly upon his youth. He was Bar Mitzvahed at Temple Beth El and was an active participant, as well as a leader, in all of its youth organizations.[4] Bernard lives today, as in his youth, in the Highlands area, close by the Temple.

Others have similar stories to tell. Alan Kaplan went to Lowell High and, upon graduation, left the city for college. Upon receiving his doctorate from Syracuse University, he returned to teach in the math department of the University of Massachusetts Lowell. Alan's grandfather, Barnet Kaplan, came as an immigrant to Lowell in the late 1800s and opened a small store. Alan's father in turn owned Fenway Clothes Shop, an upscale men's store.[5]

Gilbert Brown, a professor of nuclear engineering at the university, is the current president of Temple Beth El. He noted that there are not many cities where one can live in an area like the Highlands, where there is excellent housing available and one is able to walk to a synagogue and also find a strong Jewish presence.[6]

Gayle and Jeffrey Tye are both third generation Lowellians. They are active members of Temple Beth El. They live with their three children, ages two, six, and eleven, on Westford Street, close to Temple Beth El. Gayle tells the story that her grandfather, Harry Zeller, a furrier, came to Lowell from Austria; when his first wife died, he went back, married his deceased wife's sister and returned to Lowell. Gayle's father, Philip, is a son of that union. Jeffrey Tye is a paramedic. As a young man his father Leslie worked in the Ideal Raquet Store, a general store started by his father, Eli, who came to Lowell as an immigrant. Gayle states that they are happy to live so close to the synagogue, where it is easy for them to participate in many activities, and they are pleased that their children are able to attend the nearby Merrimack Valley Hebrew Academy where they receive both a secular and religious education. Jeffrey's sister, Paula, and her husband, Howard Flagler, a native of the old mill city of Lawrence, live nearby with their two young children. Gayle and Jeffrey's parents live in Lowell; Gayle's brother Kenneth owns Thompson Radio Service in Lowell. This extended family has deep and lasting roots in the city. Both Gayle and Jeffrey and their fathers are graduates of Lowell High School. Gayle is a 1978 graduate of the University of Lowell; Jeffrey is a 1976 graduate of the University of Massachusetts.[7]

The new young Rabbi Gordon of Temple Beth El is optimistic about the future of Temple Beth El. She points to the fact that eight very active young synagogue families have recently moved into Lowell. All live in close proximity to the synagogue. The husbands are employed in nearby high tech firms. A son of one of the families, Zachary Zaffrin, who attends Daly Middle School in Lowell, was Bar Mitzvahed on December 17, 1994. The Bar Mitzvah ceremony and celebration has proved to be an enduring milestone in Jewish life. One of Rabbi Gordon's goals is to enhance and increase attendance in the Temple's religious school.[8]

Historically, an important bond for Jews in Lowell was the plethora of Jewish-sponsored philanthropic, educational and religious organizations. There has been a decline in organizational membership and some vital former groups are now defunct. Currently, the only function of the once dynamic Pouzzner B'nai B'rith lodge is to collect dues. Throughout the country there has been a drop in memberhip in the large mass-based organizations such as B'nai B'rith, relating in part to the fact that the once attractive services they provided their members—especially the self-employed—such as death and medical benefits, now compete with insurance and pension plans that do not require organizational membership.[9]

Undoubtedly, part of the organizational decline relates to a changed lifestyle. Many women are working and there is less time for voluntary activities. It was the women who were the backbone of institutional life. These pursuits provided them opportunities to use their talents and to ensure Jewish continuity. Today, as a result of the feminist movement, many women find expression for their talents in careers that were formerly considered the province of men. The emphasis on economic independence and jobs for women results in their no longer having the need, energy or leisure for voluntary organizational acitivities.

Of the organizations that have survived and are still active, most are synagogue related. Brotherhoods and Sisterhoods are the major functioning arms of the synagogues. The decline in the number of young Jews has resulted in fewer activities for them. There is United Synagogue Youth (USY) for high school students and Kadimah (Forward) for grades 5 and 6. The emphasis in these youth groups is to provide social and cultural contacts with Jewish youths from other communities. The Lowell Chapter of Hadassah remains strong and, with its continued commitment to Israel causes, draws membership from the surrounding suburbs as well.

Unlike so many other small cities, the Jewish population of Lowell still remains concentrated around the synagogues. This highlights and makes visible their activities. As in the past, the synagogues are the paramount conservers and preservers of Jewish identity.

Throughout history an important element of Jewish life has been philanthrophy. Traditionally, charity has been viewed as an essential aspect of community organization. Jews are extolled to remember that tzedakah (Hebrew word for charity) is equated with righteousness and justice. Prosperous members are expected to perform their mitzvahs (acts of piety) through charitable deeds. The multi-service, umbrella concept of distributing charitable funds has evolved as the accepted framework for giving.[10]

An umbrella organization, the Merrimack Valley United Jewish Communities (MVUJC) was formed in 1988. Its major purpose was to coordinate Jewish activities throughout the Merrimack Valley. With the Jewish population in the region approaching 10,000 and expected to increase to 15,000 by the year 2000, it was felt that there should be a united effort to raise funds for Israel, national and local Jewish needs as well as to coordinate the celebration of Jewish community events. An additional mission was to assess the needs of the Jewish population and to develop appropriate activities and programs. With its headquarters in Andover, the goal of the MVUJC was to combine the resources of the small independent communities of Lowell, its surrounding suburbs and the cities of Lawrence, Andover and Haverhill.[11] All of the Jewish institutions in the Valley, synagogues, the Jewish community centers, Jewish schools, Jewish family service and Jewish camps, received allocations of money from the campaigns of the MVUJC.

Despite some successes, a Merrimack Valley Jewish identity did not emerge. The former Rabbi of Temple Beth El, Jonah Layman, pointed out that the agency was not working well. Problems arose because each community desired to keep funds it raised for itself and the lay leadership was not representative of the participating communities. Instead the leadership was drawn only from Andover, the most prestigious town in the area.[12]

In 1993, the MVUJC was reorganized with a new name, the Merrimack Valley Jewish Federation (MVJF). The goal of the Federation was to unite the Jewish communities of the Valley and to solidify their shared identity. It has been most successful in strengthening the programs at the Jewish Family Service. Over 200 new Americans have been resettled with housing and food assistance allowances. Also a new Jewish cultural day camp program was initiated and a hot kosher meals program started for the area elderly.[13]

The MVJF is succeeding in arranging imaginative events to promote Jewish continuity. In December 1993, the Jewish communities joined in a "First Light" celebration in which a

10 foot high, specially commissioned menorah was lit to mark the first night of Chanukah at Temple Beth El in Lowell. An intergenerational Russian American family, observing their first Chanukah in freedom, was given the honor of lighting the menorah. A chorus of children from the religious schools throughout the area led the singing of the blessings and the holiday songs. A festive family-style dinner followed the ceremony.[14]

According to the acting director, Edward Finkle, the MVJF is still struggling to raise adequate funds to support its many programs. He indicates that Lowell, faced with the demographics of a population that is not growing, is hard pressed to maintain its own institutions and is not able to contribute to the overall federation to the extent it would like.[15]

The programs initiated by the MVUJC and continued by the MVJF to foster Jewish cohesion represent part of the struggle to maintain Jewish institutions and some would say even Jewish survival in the United States. Many committed Jews fear that the effect of increased levels of education and higher status occupations, combined with a high rate of intermarriage (approaching 50 percent) and a low birth rate will result in assimilation into the surrounding dominant culture.[16] Others are less pessimistic. They believe that American Jews will never cease to exist as a distinguishable group, but will instead merely be transformed. The dichotomy of living as an American or as a Jew no longer holds. In the society as a whole, there is a weakening of the ideology of the melting pot and an upsurge of ethnic pride. There is within American Judaism acceptance of pluralism in religious observances—orthodox, conservative and reform—and also acceptance of Jews who are not religiously involved but identify as a people based on their common historical bonds. A strong return to religious customs that are symbols of a collective peoplehood has occurred. Candle lighting on Chanukah and on the Sabbath and the ceremonies accompanying circumcision, bar mitzvah, marriage, and funerals constitute a closely connected process.[17]

Since World War II, Israel has been a rallying point for Jewish survival. Now that the peace process has begun and Israel is more secure, American Jews will probably devote more attention to cultivating and celebrating their American identity and will place more emphasis on the American Jewish experience in synagogue religious schools. A question remains as to how the lack of having Israel as a unifying force for disparate Jewish communities throughout the country will affect the will of American Jews to remain Jews.

Survival of the historical Jewish community of Lowell may also be at a crossroads. Temple Beth El and Montefiore Synagogue have symbolized stability and continuity for the Jews of Lowell. If Temple Beth El moved to one of the surrounding suburbs to increase the size of its membership and attract younger families, as some have suggested, this would be a blow to the community. A precedent has been established by Temple Emanuel, in the nearby old mill city of Lawrence. When faced with declining membership, the temple moved to the adjoining suburban town of Andover. The Jewish Shtetl of Eastern Europe, self-contained as an institutionally-complete community, could not exist in the open American society but it is paramount for synagogues to remain the focal point for Jewish life in the Diaspora. In October of 1995, Temple Beth El celebrated the fortieth anniversary of the dedication of its new temple. The records of the Board of Trustees reveal the dedication and energy with which the leaders carried out their mission of erecting a modern synagogue and community center.

Ethnic and religious group identity in America has changed over time. Each group is different from when it came but each has a propensity to endure in a society which is increasingly fragmented and impersonal. Groups modify and adapt their behavior to accommodate the larger society while, at the same time, ethnic ties continue to provide a significant bond.

In Lowell, the immigrant process has endured. In July of 1982 four generations of a family of Russian Jewish immigrants who had recently settled in Lowell celebrated the retaking of the marriage vows of Raya and Boris Krasavina and their daughter and son-in-law, Inna and Edward Rozman. The wedding ceremony was performed by Rabbi James Lebeau at Temple Beth El while Inna and Eduard's fifteen year old daughter Lena, and Boris' ninety-three year old mother, Berta, looked on. With 250 people assembled, Rabbi Lebeau formally consecrated the marriage and told of the warm welcome the Krasavinas and Rozmans had received from the entire Jewish community. He proclaimed that the synagogue congregation would continue to work to secure the rescue of the three million Jews in the Soviet Union.

Both the Krasavinas in 1939 and the Rozmans in 1961 had been denied a religious Jewish wedding, since only civil ceremonies—short and formal in drab city halls—were permitted in Soviet society. The beautiful double religious ceremony, replete with standing under the huppa (a wedding canopy) and the breaking of glass, signifies that even in a moment of great joy, there was need to remember the pain in the world. The happy event concluded with resounding cheers of "Mazal Tovs" from the congregation. Berta, the great grandmother, who had been married in a ceremony with Jewish rituals in 1914 before the Russian revolution, expressed the view through an interpreter that "here is better."

The family had lived a fairly comfortable life in Leningrad but immigrated to the United States to escape religious discrimination. They settled in Lowell because Edward, a computer engineer, and Inna, a computer analyst, found jobs in the area. They expressed happiness that their daughter Lena, a student at Lowell High School, was a participant in Jewish youth groups and that as a family they could go each week to the synagogue.[18]

Russian Jews continue to be resettled in the Merrimack Valley. In 1993, with financial assistance from HIAS (the Hebrew Immigrant Aid Society) and the CJF (the Council of Jewish Federations), the Merrimack Valley communities were able to place 13 Jewish families in the valley. The resettlement services provided by the Jewish Family Service, housing and food assistance as well as access to area Jewish programs, helped ease the adjustment of these new Americans and has enabled them to participate actively in Jewish life.[19]

Today the most significant group of new immigrants are Southeast Asians, the largest segment of which are Cambodians. Since the 1970s, nearly 10,000 Southeast Asians have settled in Lowell, creating a community that has become a vital part of the city's cultural mosaic.[20]

They have come to Lowell to work. They assemble computer parts just as the earlier European arrivals came to work in the textile mills. There is now a Cambodian Temple in the area as well as Cambodian-owned food markets and restaurants. Voluntary self help social service organizations have also been established. As the Southeast Asians have begun to prosper, they are beginning to abandon old tenement dwellings and are moving into the more desirable residential areas, such as the Highlands, where the upwardly mobile Jews had settled. The Southeast Asian refugees left their homelands just as the Europeans had done almost a century earlier to escape political turmoil, poverty and suffering. Thus the multi-group heritage of Lowell is renewed. Some members of the earlier ethnic groups are disturbed that the Southeast Asians are taking over space in the over-crowded public schools and are displeased with the financial costs this entails. There is also an undercurrent of hostility against the Asians for moving out of the segregated quarters where they first dwelled. Memories are short and earlier groups forget that they also suffered prejudice and discrimination at the hands of those who had arrived before them. A new cultural influence is visibly present and sadly this undoubtedly will become a stimulus for some to leave the city for the suburbs.

For Jews the immigrant cycle has come full circle. Today, Jews in Lowell, as in the country as a whole, are comfortable in their Jewish identity. They have been accepted and have developed diversified patterns of participation in various spheres of American life as well as maintaining numerous attachments, institutional and religious to their Jewish heritage.

Notes

1. *American Jewish Year Book,* 1907-1908, Vol. 9, p. 211; 1919-1920, Vol. 21, p. 397.

2. James Higgins and Paul Marion, "Images of the New Lowell" in *The Continuing Revolution: A History of Lowell, Massachusetts,* in Robert Weible ed., Lowell Historical Society, 1991, p. 407.

3. Temple Beth El, Lowell, Massachusetts, (Unpublished) Survey of Membership, 1994.

4. Interview with Bernard Shapiro, Shirley Kolack, 1994.

5. Interview with Alan Kaplan, Shirley Kolack, 1994.

6. Interview with Gilbert Brown, Shirley Kolack, 1994.

7. Interview with Gayle Tye, Shirley Kolack, 1994.

8. Interview with Rabbi Leslie Gordon, Shirley Kolack, 1994.

9. Daniel J. Elazar, "Developments in Jewish Community Organization in the Second Post War Generation," in *American Pluralism and the Jewish Community,* Seymour Martin Lipset, ed. (New Brunswick, New Jersey: Transaction Publishers, 1990) p. 179.

10. Susan Ebert, "Community and Philanthropy," in *The Jews of Boston 1895-1995,* Jonathan D. Sarna and Ellen Smith, eds. (Boston: Combined Jewish Philanthropies, 1995) p. 211.

11. Interview with Dr. Len Gravitz, Former Director of the Merrimack Valley United Jewish Communities, Shirley Kolack, 1988.

12. Interview with Rabbi Jonah Layman, Shirley Kolack, 1994.

13. *News of the Merrimack Valley,* "Alive and Well," January 21, 1994.

14. Merrimack Valley Jewish Federation Newsletter, Spring, 1994.

15. Interview with Edward Finkle, Acting Director, Merrimack Valley Combined Jewish Federation, Shirley Kolack, March, 1995.

16. Seymour Martin Lipset, ed., *American Pluralism and the Jewish Community* (New Brunswick, New Jersey: Transaction Publishers, 1990).

17. Shmuel Eisenstadt, "The American Jewish Experience and American Pluralism" in *American Pluralism and the Jewish Community,* Seymour

Martin Lipset, ed. (New Brunswick, New Jersey: Transaction Publishers, 1990) p. 46.

18. *The Lowell Sun*, "A New Beginning," June 17, 1982.
19. Merrimack Valley Jewish Federation Newsletter, Spring, 1994.
20. James Higgins and Joan Ross, *Southeast Asians: A New Beginning in Lowell* (Lowell: Milltown Graphics, 1986).

Chapter 7

THE SAGA OF AN IMMIGRANT FAMILY

The saga of the Charles Richards family humble beginnnings in Lowell highlights the typical Jewish immigrant experience at the turn of the 20th century. Charles Richards (born Kalman Chodosz) was the oldest of eight children. He left his home in the town of Kabilnick, Lithuania, for America in 1906. He traveled by train and wagon to the port city of Hamburg, Germany, where he boarded an ocean liner. He traveled steerage class.

The ship had a kosher kitchen since so many of the passengers were Jews. There were separate sleeping quarters for men, women and children. The voyage took two weeks. Upon docking at Ellis Island, Kalman was met by an agent of the Hebrew Immigrant Aid Society who tried unsuccessfully to locate Kalman's uncle, who lived in New York City. Kalman then provided the address of a second relative, an aunt who lived in Lowell. With only ten dollars in his pocket, he was sent by boat to Fall River, Massachusetts, and then by train to Lowell.

Kalman knew only a few isolated words of English. Many Jews taught themselves some English from Yiddish-English dictionaries purchased in Europe. Prior to leaving home, Kalman had learned to sew buttons. If asked by the authorities, he was prepared to say he was a tailor. All immigrants were expected to have a trade and a relative to contact.

Upon arrival in Lowell, Kalman was taken to his aunt's home by a Jew who waited each day at the railroad station for new Jewish immigrants. A friend of Kalman's aunt and uncle got him a job at the Hamilton Manufacturing Company. Kalman walked to work and for a sixty hour per week job, he was paid $7.35. His weekly room and board were $1.25. It was customary for young single men to board with relatives. The mills were not discriminatory. Anyone who was willing to work could find a job. At that time the population of Lowell was about 100,000 and the bulk of the work force was employed in the textile mills. There were no unions.

After securing a job, Kalman's next goal was to become a citizen. He went to night school to learn enough English to be able to answer the questions about the U.S. government on the citizenship test. With two men from work as witnesses, he proudly signed his citizenship papers with the name Charles Richards. On the spot, with a judge observing, Kalman's given name and family name were changed legally. He had a cousin named Kalman who called himself Charlie and a friend named Richard—both names Kalman admired. Name changes were not unusual; Jews wanted to sound and dress like Americans. The given names of the children of immigrants were Hebrew, but the names registered at city hall would be in English. In 1909, Kalman had to leave his job at the Hamilton Mill because of an operation for appendicitis and the need to recuperate. He returned to work as a cabinet maker in Pittsfield, Massachusetts.

Kalman's parents had hoped for their gifted oldest son to become a Jewish scholar. He was sent at age eight to cheder (Jewish school) in a larger town to learn Hebrew, and then at age ten to a yeshiva (an academy for higher talmudic learning). Traditionally, European Jewish communities, no matter how poor, supported schools for study of the Talmud and Torah. Boys like Kalman would be supported for life to dedicate themselves to interpretation and commentary on religious doctrine. All this was to change in America where even the academically advanced immigrants engaged in manual labor to survive.

Kalman married Elizabeth Korotchz in 1910 (they were cousins once removed). They had known each other in the old country. They were married in a cousin's house in Worcester, Massachusetts. Couples scrimped for months to pay for weddings. After the bills were paid they often remained in debt to relatives. Kalman and Elizabeth slept their wedding night on the living room floor with twenty guests. The next morning Kalman returned to work in Pittsfield. The young couple was separated for several months until Kalman again found work in Lowell as a carpenter's helper. He earned $3.50 a week. The newlyweds rented a single room in the flat of a Jewish family; families often took in boarders to augment their income.

Kalman and Elizabeth's first child, Anne, was born in 1912 on Howard Street in the heart of the Jewish settlement. When she was three years old, the family bought a three-decker house. As was typical for many of the immigrants, they lived on the top floor and rented the lower flats. Anne recalls that the house had a yard and their relatives from New York would come to stay with them for the Jewish holidays. They relished leaving the big city for the "country."

Anne mused that in the early days all were impoverished. Mothers could not afford baby carriages. They wrapped their babies in shawls and carried them in their arms when they went out. Anne's family's flat had a bath, heat and electricity; most did not. Women used the ritual bath (mikvah) located behind a store for their regular bathing. Men struggled to make a living. Store owners worked around the clock during busy seasons. Their wives would bring supper to them to eat at work. Hyman Shafman, a cattle dealer, would walk the long distance from Lawrence to Lowell driving cows to a slaughterhouse in the Lowell area.

Extended family ties were strong and there was fierce loyalty and a deep feeling of responsibility among relatives for each other. A component of the work of the early Jewish organizations was to ensure that all Jews were adequately cared for. The Gomelos Chasidim, a loan organization, gave money to poor Jews to buy necessities. Recipients paid back twenty-five cents a week. Anne commented that everyone shared with the less fortunate and offered space for boarders. It was expected that itinerant scholars would be welcomed. On the high holidays, families volunteered to house a visiting rabbi or cantor. There was great joy in the celebration of the Sabbath and all the Jewish festivals.

Anne had two brothers, Edward, born in 1917, and Milton, born in 1922. Anne states that they were poor but did not know it. Life was hard, but they had simple pleasures. There was little room for envy; most of the immigrant families were in the same boat. Her father worked hard and would often fall asleep at the kitchen table. He went to the synagogue on Saturday afternoons and did not work on major Jewish holidays.

Anne especially delights in recalling her mother's preparation for the Friday night dinner that ushered in the Sabbath. She states, "I could smell 'Shabbas'—roasted chicken, raisin and cinnamon buns, wine and homemade root beer." The table would be set with a white cloth and glowing candles.

In the immigrant families, the oldest child was the link to adaptation to American customs. Anne's role was to instruct her mother about what was fashionable and appropriate in clothes and furniture. With her father, she discussed business and religion. For her brothers, she served as a model and a guide. Yiddish was spoken in the home but the children often answered in English. In the afternoons after public school, the children attended the Hebrew Free School, where they learned Hebrew and studied the Bible. The school was improperly named for the children paid a dollar a week fee.

During their courtship, Anne's parents had been content on Sundays to take a five cent trolley ride to nearby parks. By contrast Anne recalls that when her father got his first car—a Ford—the family drove to the north shore beaches and once stayed for a week at Revere beach. They were a literate family that read many newspapers and books. They frequented the theater and the movies. On a trip to New York to visit their uncles, they went to the Opera House and the Yiddish theater, where they saw all the famous Jewish performers—Eddie Cantor, Georgie Jessel, Sophie Tucker, Maurice Schwartz, and Mollie Picon.

The immigrant family was a beehive of activity. Mothers baked, sewed and scoured their flats, since cleanliness was next to Godliness. Preparations for Passover involved scrubbing the house inside out. Anne's mother still found time to belong to the Ladies Aid Society. Mother ran the household but the father's word was law. The children were kept busy with a variety of activities. Anne's father bought a second-hand piano so she could take lessons. She was part of a drama group at the Hebrew school, participated in a "just for fun girls group," and later became a Hadassah Bud. Her brothers had paper routes. Milton recalls that on Sundays he delivered the *New York Times*. The paper cost fifteen cents, but one customer always would give him a quarter; in Milton's eyes, this man was the most generous person in the world. Their father belonged to several self-help organizations: the Workmen's Circle, a cemetery society, and a credit union. He was also an active member of the Montefiore Synagogue.

Jewish children were encouraged to excel in school. Education was perceived as the magic wand to a better life. In America there should only be success. Anne graduated from Lowell High School in 1928. A member of the National Honor Society, she applied to Wellesley College. Since there was no vocational guidance at the high school she was not prepared for the high cost of attending an elite institution. She enrolled instead in Salem Teachers College where, after one year, she dropped out because of the Great Depression and went to work. Milton, her youngest brother, received a Ph.D. from Syracuse University. He is now a retired department head and professor emeritus from Mohawk Valley Community College in Utica, New York. Edward, the oldest brother, died in 1969. He worked with his father in the family-owned construction business (Charles Richards and Son). For while, Anne served as the firm's bookkeeper. She also sold real estate and was a resident director of the YWCA.

Jewish children were proud of their heritage. Anne loved Hebrew School and wanted to be a Hebrew teacher. Her most precious possession was a book of Yiddish stories, translated into English, that her father bought her. The Jewish neighborhood was mostly self-contained but there was a smattering of French, Greek, Finnish and Irish tenants in their midst who Anne recalls were good neighbors. Milton only remembered isolated incidents of anti-Semitism. When taunted by Christian boys with the epitaph "Christ killer," he would say his name was Sweeny and that he was a laplander. Sometimes there were language difficulties. When Anne started school, her teacher locked her in a room for disobeying. The teacher did not understand that Anne could not follow instructions because she only spoke Yiddish.

Like other Jewish parents Anne's mother and father admonished their children that Jews had to do better. If any Jew did wrong, all Jews felt collectively disgraced. When a Jewish bootlegger in New York was arrested, the Jews of Lowell felt dishonored. They also looked out for each other. They accepted the Biblical moral code, "I am my brother's keeper." During the Depression years, when business was bad, the Richards family borrowed from the credit unions to tide them over. It was understood that organizational physicians would accept whatever one could afford as payment. No one went hungry, since groceries were bought "on the book." Common expressions were "work today so tomorrow you won't do without" and "a Jew had to run twice as fast to get half as far". For the most part the young men who became lawyers worked day jobs and went to law schools at night. Some attended Lowell Textile Institute but were denied jobs in the textile industry because they were Jews. Young women who graduated from Lowell Normal School, later Teacher's College, were not hired to teach. Anne recalled having only a Jewish substitute teacher, Rose Nyman, who taught French.

Children respected their parents and did not talk back to them. The patriarchal tradition was strong. Milton noted that he never thought of his father as a greenhorn; he was proud of his father's Talmudic knowledge. However, when he went to the movies with his mother, she would sob loudly at the sad parts and he would cover his embarrassment by laughing even though he felt like crying too. Anne found her mother less old fashioned than her father, who hated for his wife to use lipstick and powder—but she did anyway, for weddings and other special occasions.

Since the Jewish population was small and relatively young, acculturation occurred rapidly. Immigrant men shaved off their beards and discarded their tales-kotn (a four cornered tasseled undergarment worn by religious Jews). Wives stopped wearing sheitls (wigs worn after marriage). When Kalman Chodosz applied for his first job in the mill, the doctor who examined him advised him to throw away his tales-kotn. Within two months of leaving his orthodox home in Lithuania, he had removed the most distinctive marks of his orthodoxy—beard, earlocks and tales-kotn. Jewish children were exposed to new customs in the public schools. They in turn shared these experiences with their parents. Thus the schools functioned as an adaptation mechanism for the entire family.

Anne remembered that as a young child at school and at play, she was friendly with children from other ethnic groups. However, neither children, as they grew older, nor their parents, socialized or attended the celebrations of the other groups. It was expected that Jews would marry Jews and that girls would remain virgins until marriage. Her mother admonished her in Yiddish "Dem kugel halt men far shabas" (you keep the pudding for the sabbath). Most marriage partners were either from Lowell families or from the surrounding towns. Anne dated young men from Lowell, Lawrence, Haverhill and Worcester.

Anne married Max Baskin in Lowell in 1933. He was born in New York but grew up in Worcester, Massachusetts, where other family members had settled. His parents came from Eastern Europe. Max aspired to become a dentist but he did not have the money for dental school. He went to work as a soap salesman for Fels-Naphta. Shortly after his marriage, Max lost his job because of the Depression. After fasting and praying all day on Yom Kippur, he went for a job interview that evening. It was successful, and he rose to the position of the comptroller for the Middlesex Plumbing Supply and Hardware Company.

The couple's first son, Marshall, born in 1938, died tragically at the age of thirteen not long after his Bar Mitzvah. He drowned in a summer camp accident. Marshall had been an honor student. Their second son, David, was born in 1948. As did their mother, both sons attended the Lowell public schools. David graduated from the University of Massachusetts Amherst and went on to receive a law degree from George Washington University in Washington, D.C. He is now a trial lawyer for the U.S. Department of Labor in Boston. He lives with his wife, Constance, and two children in Acton, Massachusetts.

Over the years, the Baskin family maintained strong ties to the Jewish community. They moved into the Highlands area and were enthusiastic members of Temple Beth El, where both their sons, Mitchell and David, were Bar Mitzvahed. David recalls that his entire social life and after-school activities revolved around the Jewish Community Center at the Temple. Anne was active in the sisterhood of the Temple and as a volunteer for Jewish service organizations such as Haddassah. In her later years, she taught English to Southeast Asian refugees at the International Institute in Lowell.

Grandmother Elizabeth Richards died in 1963. She is remembered as an extremely loving and warm person who always helped those in need. She followed orthodox Jewish practices strictly, maintaining a kosher household by observing dietary rules. Charles Richards, the grandfather, died in 1977. As was the custom for caring for aged parents, he lived with his daughter Anne after the death of his wife. A pious man, he never worked on the Sabbath and regularly attended Montefiore Synagogue services. He was honored by the synagogue for his lifelong participation shortly before he died. Edward Richards, the oldest son, died in 1969. His wife Madeline lives in Nashua, New Hampshire. The youngest son, Milton Richards, is retired and lives with his wife Adele (whose family also has Lowell roots) in Fort Myers, Florida. There are several children and grandchildren of the Richards brothers. Anne Baskin, who is 83, has lived for the past several years at the Hebrew Rehabilitation Center in Roslindale, Massachusetts. Her husband, Max Baskin, died in 1961.

The Richards and Baskin families provide an example of family continuity from the old world to the new. They were able to simultaneously obtain a measure of personal fulfillment while adapting to a new society, preserving their religious heritage and group identity. First and second generations deferred their dreams; only the third generation fulfilled their goals.

Note: Material for this chapter is based on interviews with members of the Richards and Baskin families, as well as family letters. The unpublished paper written by David Baskin, "The Jews in Lowell, 1905-1918," was also used as a reference.

PHOTOGRAPHS

Original Jewish Cemetery (Brith Abraham) in Pelham, New Hampshire, established in 1893

Photographs 85

A Russian Jewish Couple: Courtesy of Lowell Museum

Montefiore Synagogue on Howard Street as urban renewal begins circa 1960. Anshe Sfard Synagogue on Howard Street circa 1907.

Lowell Young Men's Hebrew Association, 1913

Members of Lowell's Morgan (sic) David (Star of David) Baseball Team circa 1925

The Highland Club purchased in 1926 for the first home of the Lowell Hebrew Community Center and Temple Beth El on Princeton Boulevard. Courtesy of *Lowell Sun*.

New Lowell Hebrew Community Center and Temple Beth EL dedicated 1955, Princeton Boulevard, Highlands, on site of Old Highland Club

Street procession from Howard Street to new Montefiore Synagogue on Westford Street, September, 1971

New Montefiore Synagogue on Westford Street, Highlands, Dedicated 1970

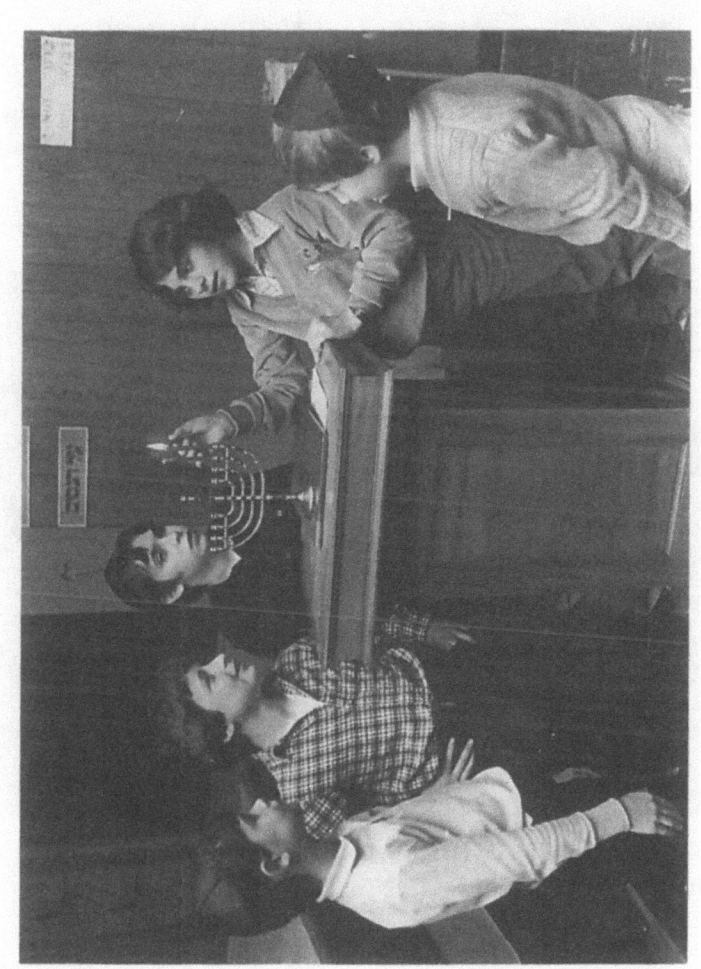

Lighting the Chanukah Menorah, Temple Beth El Religious School Students, 1980. Courtesy of *Lowell Sun*

Ceremony 1981 at Lowell City Hall celebrating the Founding of Israel, 1947. Courtesy of *Lowell Sun*

Rabbi Epstein reading from a Holocaust Torah, Temple Beth El, 1986

Passover Seder Table, Family of Rabbi Shlomo Hochberg of Montefiore Synagogue, 1989. Courtesy of *Lowell Sun*.

INDEX

Abels, Franklin 2
Abraham Lincoln Elementary
 School 11
Aleph Zadek Aleph (AZA) 22, 49
America (poem) 50
American Jewish Year Book 63
American Red Cross 26
Andover 14
Ansin, Harold 34
Ansin, Joseph 35
Ansin, Lawrence 34
anti-Semitism 3, 7, 8, 17, 36, 51,
 53, 79
Arbeiter Ring (Workmen's Circle)
 21, 54, 79
Austria 25
Ayer 14

Banks, Mendel 58
Barlofsky, Abraham 10
Barlofsky, Maurice 10, 27
Baskin, Constance 81
Baskin, David 81
Baskin, Marshall 81
Baskin, Max 81, 82
Bass's Cloak and Suit Company
 32
Belvidere district 14
Ben-Gurion, David 22
Benjamin S. Pouzzner Lodge of
 B'nai B'rith 22, 38, 53,
 55, 67
Bernstein, Albert 37
Bernstein, Barbara 13, 37
Bernstein Shoes 37

Beth El Sisterhood 13
Birke, Nathan 43
Birke, Sally 43
Birke, Szifra 44
Blue Room Nightclub and Restau-
 rant 34
B'nai B'rith Youth Organization
 (BBYO) 22, 49
B'nai Israel Society 8
Boott Mills 12, 28
Boston 3, 8, 13, 44
Boston Globe 34
Boston University 40
Bourgeois, Homer 42
Braverman, Edwin 38
Brown, Gilbert 65

Callaway, Cab 34
Cantor Insurance Company 27,
 35
Cantor, Jacob 35
Cantor, James 35
Cantor, William 27, 35
Capitol Theater 33
Chaloff, Judith Green 49
Chanukah 56
Chelmsford, Massachusetts 14,
 19, 38
Chevra Kadisha 19
Chodosz, Kalman 80
Chosiod, Miriam 33
Christian Front 53
Civil War 14
Coburn, Frederick 52
Cohen, A. Paul 15, 27

Cohen, Esther 10, 39
Cohen, Max 10, 39
Cohen, Nathan 11, 13, 40
Colonial Theater 33
Community Center Players 24
Congregation Shalom 14
Coughlin, Father Charles 53
Council of Jewish Federations
    (CJF) 71
Cross Point 63
Cushing, Cardinal Richard 53

Daly Middle School 66
Diaspora 3
Digital Equipment Corporation 36
Don't Foreclose on Us 50
Draperies Design 37

Educational Alliance 22
Eisenhower, Dwight D. 22
Ellis Island 75

Factory Shoe Outlet 37
Faith Alive (radio program) 19
Fenway Clothes Shop 65
Ferman, Joseph 37
Finkle, Edward 69
five-cent club (see Israel Brotherhood Lodge)
Flagler, Howard 66
Flagler, Paula 66
Fleet Bank 42
Fort Devens 26
French Canadians 2
French immigrants 14

Garnick, David 37
Garnick, Paul 37
Garnick, Robert 37
Garnick, Sylvia 37
Gemiluth Chassodim Society 20
Gintler, Everett 19
Genesis 1948 23
George Washington University 81
Germany 25
Glassman, Norman 33

Glazer, Libby 37
Glazer, Melvin 37
Goldberger, Rabbi Chaim 59
Goldman, Frank 22, 43, 50
Goldman, Robert 43
Goldman, Rose 23, 50
Gomelos Chasidim 77
Gordon, Leslie 60, 66
Greek immigrants 14
Greenberg, Esrael 34
Greenberg, Max 25
Grey's Furniture Company 33

Hadassah 23, 67, 81
Hadassah Buds 23, 49, 78
Hale-Howard Street area 7, 9, 13
Hamilton Manufacturing Company 76
Hand, Learned 43
Harvard University Law School 43
Haverhill, Massachusetts 21
Hebrew Free Loan Societies 20
Hebrew Free School 28, 78
Hebrew Immigrant Aid Society
    (HIAS) 21, 71, 75
Hertzberg, Arthur 3
Highland Club 12, 18, 23
Highland Credit Union 21
Highland Congregational Church 12
History of Lowell and Its People 52
Hockberg, Karen 60
Holocaust 26, 43, 51
Holtz, Jackson 55
Howe, Richard 59
Hyman, Max 36

Ideal Credit Union 21
Independent Lodge of Brith Abraham 19
Industrial Removal Board 7
International Institute (Lowell) 11, 81
Irish immigrants 2, 14, 52
Israel 22, 23, 26, 51, 53, 68, 69
Israel Brotherhood Lodge 10

Index

Jacob Ziskin Foundation 41
Jacobson, Eddie 23
Jewish War Veterans 24, 25
Joan Fabric 34
Johnson Act 2

Kadimah 67
Kahn, Gabriel 28
Kaplan, Alan 65
Kaplan, Barnet 65
Kenngott, George 9
Khilos Jacobe 11
Klesaris, Stella XI
Knopf, Sam 33
Korotchz, Elizabeth 76
Krasavina, Boris 70
Krasavina, Raya 70
Kurzman, Daniel 23

Ladies' Hebrew Helping Hand
    Society 20
Landsmanschaften organizations
    21
Lawrence, Massachusetts 21
Layman, Jonah 68
Lebeau, Rabbi James 70
Lemkin, Herman 32
Lemkin, Morris 32
Lemkin's Women's Apparel 32
Levi, Harry 18
Levine, Aaron 37
Levine, Allan 38, 51
Levine, Mark XI
Levine, Morey 38
Levine, William 38
Levine, William 26, 27
Levy, Ida 29
Lithuania 2, 65, 75, 80
Lowell Business Directory of 1892
    39
Lowell Community Chest Association 38
Lowell Credit Union 21
Lowell Five Cent Savings Bank 39
Lowell General Hospital 38
Lowell Grammar School 40
Lowell Harvard Club 39

Lowell Hebrew Community Center
    25, 38
Lowell Hebrew Independent Club
    20
Lowell High School 11, 40, 43,
    44, 65, 79
Lowell Historic Preservation
    Commission XI
Lowell Jewish Community Center
    18, 23, 26
Lowell Lion's Club 27, 38
Lowell, Massachusetts
    decline of commerce 35
    early history 1, 7
    industrial development 14
    observance of religious holidays
        56-59
    occupational patterns 31
    politics 27
    population growth 2, 14, 36
    revival 37, 63
    urban renewal 13
Lowell National Historical Park
    3, 13
Lowell Memorial Auditorium 34
Lowell Normal School (later
    Teacher's College) 36, 80
Lowell Rotary Club 27
Lowell Sun 22, 43
Lowell Sunday Telegram News 22,
    34
Lowell Technological Institute 41
Lowell Textile Institute 65, 80
Lowell United Fund 27
Lowell United Jewish Appeal 26,
    38
Lowell Vox Populi 8

Marlborough Hotel 23
Massachusetts Institute of Technology (MIT) 65
McIntyre Synagogue 17
McIntyre Shul 11
Merrimack Cemetery Corporation
    38
Merrimack Paper Tube Corporation 40

Merrimack River 1, 7, 8
Merrimack Valley 1, 13
Merrimack Valley Hebrew Academy 18, 42
Merrimack Valley Jewish Federation (MVJF) 68
Merrimack Manufacturing Company 9, 10, 14, 34, 41
Merrimack Valley United Jewish Communities (MVUJC) 68
Middlesex Company 2
Middlesex Paper Tube Company 37
Middlesex Plumbing Supply and Hardware Company 81
Mitre Corporation 36
Model Cities project 36
Mogan Cultural Center XI
Montefiore, Sir Moses 11
Montefiore Synagogue 11, 12, 13, 18, 19, 40, 42, 59, 70, 79, 82
Mogan David (baseball team) 24
Mogan Cultural Center 43
Mohawk Valley Community College 79
Mooney, Cardinal Edward 53
Moore, Fanny 36
Muskovitz, Sidney 35

Nazis 26
National Automotive Trade Association 39
New York Times 79
Newman's Clothing 32
Northeastern University 41
Nyman, Rose 80
NYNEX 64

Office of Price Administration 27
orthodoxy 19

Palestine 23
Palefsky, Morris 26, 34, 57
Paley, Bert 57

Pan American Exposition 25
Parrot Hat 37
Passover 56
Pattek, Nina XI
Pawtucket falls 1
Pearl Harbor 25
Pelham, New Hampshire 10, 19
Pilot (newspaper) 53
Poland 2
Polish immigrants 14
Porton, Jerry 37
Pouzzner, Benjamin A. 22, 34

Record of a City 9
Reeves, Alvin 19
Rex Ballroom 24
Rialto Theater 33
Richards, Adele 82
Richards, Anne 77, 82
Richards, Charles 75, 82
Richards, Edward 77, 82
Richards, Elizabeth 82
Richards, Milton 77, 82
Rindler, Sidney 58, 59
Rogers, Edith Nourse 28
Rosengard, Reuben 36
Rosh Hashonah 57
Roosevelt, Franklin Delano 28, 54
Rozman, Edward 70
Rozman, Inna 70
Rozman, Lena 70
Russia 2
Russian Anshe Sfard 11

Salem Teacher's College 79
Sandler, Benjamin 24, 36, 39, 40, 53
Shafman, Hyman 77
Shapiro, Bernard 65
Shapiro, Diana 65
Shapiro, Morris 65
Shapman, Hyman 51
Shoshana 49
Silver, Nat 33
Silverblat, Bennett 10
Silverblat, Samuel 10

Social Justice (newspaper) 53
Solomont, Alan 34, 42
Solomont, Ahron 34
Solomont, David 34
Solomont, Elkeh 41
Solomont, Jay 34
Solomont, Joseph 33, 41
Solomont, Meyer 34, 41
Solomont, Sy 34, 41
Solomont, Todras 41
Sons of Abraham 39
Star of Bethlehem 9
Strand Theater 33
Styman, Pearl 50
Succoth 57
Suffolk Knitting Company 15, 27
Syracuse University 65, 79

Talmud Torah Hall 20
Talmud Torahs (Hebrew schools) 28
Temple Beth El 12, 13, 14, 18, 19, 23, 34, 38, 40, 43, 49, 50, 55, 60, 65, 69, 70, 81
Temple Emanuel 12, 19, 70
Tewksbury State Hospital 20
The Jews in America 3
Towers Motor Parts Corporation 26, 37
Truman, Harry 22
Tye, Gayle 66
Tye, Jeffrey 66
Tyler, David Gardner 12
Tyler, John 12

U.S. Department of the Interior XI
United Fund 39
United Hebrew Charities of New York 7, 8
United Nations 23
United Service Organization (USO) 26

Union National Bank of Lowell 38, 42
United Synagogue Youth (USY) 67
Universalism 3
University of Massachusetts Amherst 81
University of Massachusetts Lowell 13, 14, 36, 42, 64, 66

Van Greenby, David 25, 56
Van Greenby, Donald 25, 34
Vesper Country Club 27, 38
Victory Tower Memorial Palace 33

Wang Laboratories 36, 63
War Production Board 27
Warren, Joseph 17, 26, 50
Westford 14
Willow Manor Nursing Home and Retirement Center 13, 34, 42
Wise, Rabbi Steven 55
Witty, Abraham 18
Wolfson, Elias 17
World War 1 2, 12, 25
World War 2 12, 13, 25, 53

Yorick Club 27, 38
Young Men's Hebrew Association 22, 24, 25
Young Women's Hebrew Association 22, 24

Zaffrin, Zachary 66
Zeller, Harry 66
Zionism 26
Zionist Organization of America (ZOA) 53
Zion's Banner 9
Ziskind, David 34, 40
Ziskind, Jacob 34, 40